Poets Speaking to Poets

Echoes and Tributes

Edited by

Nicholas Fargnoli and Robert Hamblin

Ars Omnia Press

ISBN: 9798757871110

ArsOmni Press
SophiaOmni Publishing

Visit our website at:
www.sophiaomni.org

To Michael Patrick Gillespie, brilliant colleague, exemplary scholar, and generous friend.

Nicholas Fargnoli

For Harvey Hecht, colleague, editor, and friend.

Robert Hamblin

Contents

Introduction

Poets Speaking to Poets: Echoes and Tributes presents a collection of contemporary poems celebrating two common and enduring features of a poetic tradition reaching back to the ancient Greeks and Romans: *imitation* and *tribute*.

By definition tribute evokes praise of some sort or another, but imitation is not so accommodating. It carries multiple meanings including disparaging ones. Parody, burlesque, and satire can all imitate while at the same time ridicule and mock. Imitation can also be so broad that it is rendered meaningless and merely point to generic forms. Epics, odes, sonnets, blank verse, sestinas and so forth once introduced are stylistically imitated, adapted, and even innovatively transformed over and over again. Our choice of the word echoes avoids both negative connotations and generic vagueness that can at times be associated with imitation. Echoes embrace a range of characteristics unique to a poet's style.

This volume offers another example of the prominent contemporary critical concept of *intertextuality*, that is, the way separate literary texts may be read as dialogue (hence our title, *Poets Speaking to Poets*), with the language, characterizations, themes, and styles of one providing clarification and insight on the other. Building upon and expanding the age-old literary device of allusion, intertextuality brings together discreet texts in a reciprocal manner that provides illuminating perspectives on each. T.S. Eliot once remarked (in "Tradition and the Individual Talent") that "No poet, no artist of any art, has his complete meaning alone," and his poem, "The Waste Land," is a virtual textbook on the manner in which past writers influence present ones. But contemporary practitioners of intertextual readings look backward as well as forward. Not only is the current poem enriched by reference to a previous one, but fresh insights and newer perspectives are offered on the source poem.

Each poet in this collection has contributed two poems, one in the style of another poet and one as a tribute to a poet. The contributors come from all parts of the country, from the Heartland and Hawaii, from the west coast to south Florida, from New York City to San Antonio, and beyond. One currently lives in Indonesia and another lived for a time in India. Imitating and paying tribute to poets from the ancients to our contemporaries still writing today, the contributors in this anthology remind us that poetry is not only the oldest of literary forms but also one with a perduring universal appeal. This volume acknowledges and celebrates that appeal.

Nicholas Fargnoli and Robert Hamblin

Part I: Echoes

For Me, Talking With God

Sarah Dickenson Snyder

after Anne Sexton

God has a green voice, the shades
and waves I see from a deck in Vermont,

the leaf lingering bordering the field that holds
a pond, the wispy-end stalks too long, needing cutting

by the tractor that creates concentric paths in the grass.
Green is everywhere, even on the surface —

a reflected wall of branches, arms entwined. And there's the green-
throated duck skirting and skimming, the busy feet

invisible like my parents' ashes
settled under the clean water.

Yorick Replies to Hamlet

Joseph Stanton

after Robert Browning

You pity me, my callow prince,
young as you are and melancholy?
I lived for jokes, as you well know,
one joyous gibe after another,
but being dead is not as bad
as thinking of it, and yet
this grimmest of consummations
is never sincerely wished for,
even by you, despite your pale
and whining fatalistic
grumblings, devout or otherwise.

Listen to me, Hamlet, sage advice
from my skull to yours; the dead king lies.
The only poison in the ear
is his words in yours. Your uncle
loved your mother, it is true;
but so did many others.
Even I might be your father.
Who could blame her? The king
loved only soldiery
and beardless soldiers; that's why he
comes now crying to you, young man,
to bring him his consolation.
He wants to see the blood flow, hot and red,
and you, fair prince, will be among the dead.

If you could hear my ghosted voice
over the sad clamor of your mind,
I could save you yet, but the stars
have scripted an ill-fortuned end.

One last bone I have for you
of my gravest common sense,
a parting word to the wise enough
to stay alive: all skulls smile
and all ghosts lie. The rest is silence.

Dead Letter to Elizabeth Bishop

Todd Davis

after Elizabeth Bishop

You wrote the mist
was *like rotting snow-*
ice sucked away
almost to spirit,

and you were right,
all this white
thawed and frozen,
thawed and snowed on,
and today drifting up
in melting fog.

We haven't seen
bare earth
for five months,
and the river
only opens
where the springs
melt ice.

We fish these holes,
eat enough
to keep body knit.

The soul slips
its fingers
from the wool
of winter, unshucks
and floats above
the sleeping frames
of flesh, the idle
smell of sex.

In the slowing
streams of blood
a woman dreams
of a daughter
and full cupboards,

a man of a boy
who might help
with fences
and spring
planting.

After Anyte

Sandy Feinstein

Orange, black, white cats
manged and feral
range Zeus's Temple for voles
among its colossal columns.

Thundering its losses,
the oracle is heavy rain
mourning eroded rock
at Delphi.

St. Paul has the last laugh
at Corinth, flattened
fountains and barren shops
scatter of marble stones.

Hydra's batteries curl round
like a donkey's shoe thrown
as it hoofs narrow streets
toting foreigners in winter rain.

If a dime drops in Epidaurus
and is heard in the theatre,
what does it mean today
in a pocketful of change?

Stone lions meet at Mycenae
guarding broken marble
below and beyond, the dead
remembered in towering tombs.

A Sort of Benediction on the House

Kevin McIlvoy

after Miller Williams

Well.
You seemed to me like you would listen.

A bobdamn poem is a hard thing to explain.

The people here say to me, You're more like
yourself than you think, and, You want what you need
without much needing what you want, and, Go to
a goddamn doctor when your heart is broke, B, and,
Won't you sit somewhere else for once?

And, You're not helping or hurting anyone, the
people here say who know me anyway, Did we
ever say we gave a shit about poetry?

I wanted you to tell me what the fuck I
had in mind needing to talk to H about her
newest ones, Lucinda Williams' songs made with
Charles Lloyd & The Marvels — you heard of them or him?

I told H, I said, It's like she sat down with her
father Hank, I mean Miller, and made these recordings.
And do you remember I had never heard of
her until you made me listen on a long drive
together, Cruces to Tucson, late September
2001, going to visit Steve Orlen,
who at that time was so not dying that his sly
grin could slip us into his microclimate,
I mean his parable, I mean his bobdamn poem.

H's car had no air conditioning, had one working
speaker, a barely functioning tape-player

that he actually called his "stereo system."
Did I think he cared? Did I?
I said to him, when I heard her steel wheels on a
gravel road, that I guessed I had never listened to dead
girls like I should have, their voices coming from blade
grinders and wood chippers and prom-dress shredders
after trips to the wordshed for proper
beatings. I asked H, *Did you ever have a wood*
burner as a kid? H said, Nine years old —
you could write words, hear them hiss — came with ten
sheets of balsa thin as playing cards and
the same size — adults of that generation
wanted us to injure ourselves, don't you
think? Mightaswell've given us —

I said, Chainsaws.

— Carruth Brand McCullochs, said *H, Dangerous.*

I said, I'm telling you you've got to hear this:
Lloyd playing his flute and his tenor sax and the
tarogato, a kind of saxaclarinetophone
made from the same mourning-shawl-mud as Williams'
voice. I said, H. H. I want us to take a
drive — can't we go someplace hours away and listen
to this surrendering together? She's out on
the edge of alone, she's big-ugly as a hell
bone, she's never been able to completely,
really die the ways she does on these recordings,
these giant mispositioned chainsaw carvings.

I love that — like H, at the end of life, at
the very end, was going to interrupt the
ride for the sake of music I recommended,
one friend of so many, and the least alive
of all of them. I love that. I love that. I do.

Like H was going to listen with me
listening like never before, like he could
ignore his own best instincts calling or
his mother or father or anyone
else who wouldn't get this obsessiveness
that two young musicmeasled boys had who could
not avoid contact with contagion or would
not, like we were altered boys in The First Church
of the Attic with the album doing its
crackle-spinning poem-making and us starting
it over at the widest outer ring, landing
like sonicnauts on LP planetoids
and lifting off but orbiting the counter-
spinning, roiling atmospheres of singing.

The drinks are not on me if that's what you thought. I
thought you people could be kind to my kind, that's all —
what harm have I done sitting here at this well — not
myself since H's death, undiagnosable
as an asymptomatic poem located among strangers
in an empty stadium where a drone circles
the mustardy, greased, beery hangdog faces in
the stands, and circles the pennants and seedpod crown
of lights and the last row of nosebleed seats, circles
the outfield walls, surveils the long leather fingers
of the players' gloves held up in the air by the
hatreds, the hopes of unmanacled fans who have
thrown their hotpassion-pink foam hands down and have
gone before the last inning, not one left, not one
lingering, not one at the well-lit concession
stands, the bathrooms, section railings or Exit
drains. Could that be what a damned poem does or
is — my guess is as good as yours, and I guess,
I guess, a spaceship-type drone is the sort of thing
I mean, air-riding in dragonfly down-quivers
and head-fakes, tagging the bases on the diamond
and rereading the cleat dust marking them before

refocusing the poem-cam so it can steal
second, touch-land and overshoot third, set down on
home plate in a quiet mode, blade barely cycling,
waiting for the team to begin flying from the
full dugout to celebrate the season-ender.

I haven't bought a round — you know I wish I had
that kind of cash, that kind of credit or wallet
or sense of fair play — you know that, people, you know
because you're mine, aren't you, you're my people.

I love that.

Traveling
Robert Hamblin

—For Kaye

after John Donne

We need no map
or guidebook
for this journey.
Or rather, we'll be
each other's map
and guide.

Let our hands be feet
to stroll through all the hills
and valleys of our passion,
north, south, east, and west,
and every compass point
in between.

Let my eyes be sun,
warming you along footpaths
and rippling streams
to waterfalls hidden
within the deep woods.

Let your lips be wind,
cooling my body
on a grassy knoll
where we linger
to feast on cheese and wine.

Let our hearts be birds,
diving into the lake
and flying to the tops
of the highest trees.

Let our thoughts be clouds,
floating, rising,
pure white and speechless,
against the blue sky.

Let our souls be air,
melted, fused, invisible,
contented to be joined together,
forever.

Things Are Never the Same
Jack Ridl

after Mary Ruefle

Let's say you like birdhouses. Let's say
you like birds, too. Roaming through
the antique mall that took over
the Church of the Last Christ Jesus
that had taken over the Spinning Lights
Roller Rink where twenty years ago
you wished you didn't have a lisp and
didn't have to skate alone when
the baritone crooned, "Alllllllll
skate. All skate," let's say you find
a two story Victorian perfect for wrens
or goldfinches, a stern Shaker round
walled barn just right for grackles,
two slant-roofed boxes made to welcome
wood ducks, seven gourds that will sway
from branches rocking chickadees,
juncoes, and nuthatches, and a high-rise
apartment for a cult of purple martins.
What is one more or more to hang
with the others hooked over the branches
of the maples, oaks, hemlocks, birches,
sycamores, and your one curly willow?

Josey's Ear
David Cravens

after Dr. Seuss

into the refrigerator
I peer
for a beer —
& see an ear

oh dear

should I bury the ear?
here?
it's been near a year

no — I dare not bury the ear
for fear
I may shed a tear

& I hear
that others may jeer
or leer — or sneer

or perhaps think I'm queer

so I'll steer clear —

maybe next year
I'll bury the ear

Burnt Offering
Nicholas Fargnoli

after T. S. Eliot

Between the intent and interpretation
What might have been heard
Was said
Between the echo and communication
What might have been said
Died to the unspoken word
To the gesture and mystery of hope
What might have been heard or said
Lies buried in muted ashes
That silence brings.

The hour of grief and waiting
Temple and garden
Harvest from the sacred land
Ritual and belief
Commingled sacrifice of freedom and sorrow
The sadness of blessing
From faith's other hand
Covenant blood
Spilt within time's spiritual desire
Sleep without dreams
Where voices are calling
Trammelled by confusion
And burning with fire.

Red and White:
Can the Blues Be Far Behind?

James Penha

A Song of Myself
after Walt Whitman

I believe a leaf of grass is no less than the journey-work of the stars. . .

Despite all customs and agricultural prohibitions,
I carried one August a sack of shady Kentucky bluegrass seed
from a K-Mart in New York to our island retreat
east of Bali where beneath the coconut palms
and mango trees the native greengrass wouldn't grow as lushly
as my love for Indonesia and its son who loves me.
But every pip we plant in this tropical soil grows —
even the unintended pit germinates —
and so by October the sun stroked our garden bluegreen
for aboriginal roots foliated too to vie with K-leaves
even as we heard the bombs rumble right across the strait
a tsunami of terror one year, one day, one hour after
my other isle's, Mannahatta's, bluest morning.

Walt Whitman, a Kosmos, of Manhattan the son.

The terror that blasted me from Manhattan
twelve years ago uniformed in Customs slash
Immigration under signs of Welcome
lying to a young dark man daring
to love across borders. He
was not wanted here
the Law declared
my desire out
of order.

I am given up by traitors,
I talk wildly, I have lost my wits, I and nobody else am the greatest
traitor . . .

Out of order and out of motherland we live
amidst a moveable feast,
this land and sea, Walt:
hawkers of meatball soup,
bats and balls of fruit,
peanut sauced salads, young coconut milk,
syruped ice, clove-scented cigarettes and kebabs,
fried dough, fired chicken,
live goats and cows
and everywhere happy soda — a Ninth
Avenue street festival on every street
every night on every island

> *All this I swallow, it tastes good, I like it well, it becomes mine,*
> *I am the man, I suffer'd, I was there.*

We live
in sight of democratic vistas younger than America's was to Walt
where the shaman prays to Jesus,
where the boy in the Osama tee wears a New York Yankee cap,
where the transsexual songstress pilgrimed in Mecca,
where the Iraqi refugee cannot believe I oppose a war
that he is hungry for,
where the Afghans waiting for Australia to freeze over
before they are allowed in wonder
why I would possibly live in the developing world for love
or money,
where the handlers of the land and the oil
have dealt a few handsome blackjacks
and millions of losing hands
where the shadows of the puppets loom large.

> *Wherever he goes men and women accept and desire him,*
> *They desire he should like them, touch them, speak to them, stay with*
> *them.*

Under the red and white flag of this country,

we bleed unashamedly,
the shaman and me and the Christian
and me and Osama's Yankee fan and me
and the transsexual and me and the refugees
and, yes, the dealers and the blackjacks
and the losers and the puppets
are me and the son of Indonesia
who go with the team, Walt,
and Walt, you are me
and Bali and Manhattan
following me everywhere
with your free verse and green grass
and the blues.

The Treat
Judith Sanders

after Sharon Olds

At the ice cream counter the ample waitress
keeps scooping samples I don't want.
First a flavor called White House,
created by Granddad after he went to DC
at cherry blossom time. No self-respecting
tree ever produced fruits like these
red plastic chews, studding cold cotton balls
soaked in cough syrup. She chatters
about guys who stagger in for a beer,
about her favorite phosphate: Hershey's,
seltzer, scoops of vanilla. I can feel myself
getting fat. She offers yet another spoon:
an Alpine peak of Blueberry Creme. It tastes
like shaving lather. But she's friendly,
it's a Tuesday afternoon; a few stools over,
an elderly couple admire their twin
dripping sundaes. She strews rainbow
jimmies for a prancing toddler, even
adorns the dish with a shimmery ribbon.
The bell over the door jingles; in strut
stubbled guys in overalls, catcalling
for triple dips of *White House*.

                                    Sheltered
by my shoulder, my slender son solemnly
celebrates turning thirteen-and-a-half
with what to him is the tallest, creamiest
of chocolate milkshakes, the kind the angels
must sip in heaven. One taste and I feel
like rushing to the dentist, but my son
can handle sweetness. Happy half-birthday,
son. You're halfway between so many

things. I count out bills, stack emptied
spoons. Soon you'll suck up the last drops
and leave, the bell jingling behind you.

Frontline Hero
Dee Allen

after Langston Hughes

He used to be a soldier
With a camp to protect.
Now he's a dirty, penniless man
That gets no respect.

He once carried a machine gun
And fought the enemy on the frontline.
What's his mission these days?
Keeping the cold off his behind.

He even saved another soldier
Before bombs could cut the cord.
Now he's begging for spare change,
Only to be ignored.

Decorated war hero
Returns back home
Since half of his
Brigade is dead –

Falling fast
Asleep on the sidewalk
Reliving the war
Inside his head.

Pareidolia
Timothy Gauss

after Sylvia Plath

The smell of cherry wood
Carries me to this place
'Like a season lying itself down'

Between barstool and autumn
A bartender ancient
As if these walls were built around him

Relic and wise
Burley and punk
Typewriter skin and ink tongue

Somewhere between drone and
Repetition sits a traveler
A silhouette made of corners

A shadow encased in smoke
A damp vibration
Pull of ash

Ember fingertips
Eyes of light —
Pure light

He pretends not to notice the precise tap of foot
Each second — like clockwork
Faint

A gift, unasked
On the house
When morning light

Remembers only footsteps
That carried him in—
Wisps of air

Shall I compare thee to a summer's day?
Carolyn Martin

after Billy Collins

I better not. You'd boil at the thought.
Might I entice you toward an early spring?
You could explode through thaw like daffodils
or strut with stellar jays around our yard.
Or, how about the star magnolia tree
that beats out cherry, plum, forsythia
each year and risks a frost to be the first?
Something in you, my dear, desires to lead,
can't bear the thought of standing second best.

But let me clarify: there's just no way
you are the mower needing sharpening
nor peat that rests behind our garden shed
nor surly rains that shut a gardener in.
You've gleaned — withstanding twenty years
of partnering — I am the mower dulled
from summer's wear. I am the peat that waits
its spread as soon as coastal storms abate.
And, if you wish, I'd even be the shed.
Something in me feels worthy to protect.

But if these images still needle you
and you'd prefer the echo of a smile,
organic food consuming kitchen shelves,
the copper tint you splashed across our walls,
please humor me. Jot down on sticky notes
the things that speak to you of you. Arrange
them like perennials in tidy rows
near my writing pad and coffee cup.
I am an unlined page and cooling brew.

Song of the Sirens of Life
D. R. James

after Marvin Bell

The domestic smile of snow,
the anonymous kindness of white,
the imagination of the mouth,

the grains of ebbing desire,
those inaudible explosions,
those nominal pleasures,

the churches of the vapor —
my tired mother finally
flew; what she had chosen

mimicked a parachute. Not
a soul had bewitched her,
but signaled safety, so sure.

Corruption
Sheri Vandermolen

after Lawrence Ferlinghetti

Pity the nation . . .
Whose sages are silenced
*   — Lawrence Ferlinghetti*

obstruction
privation
protraction
deception
disruption
induction
subversion
ignition
sedition
explosion
fruition
perception
division
perversion
retraction
revision
precision
collusion
succession
duration

Untitled
Anne Harding Woodworth

after Emily Dickinson

Dear Autumn — Come in —
I got your letter —
How happy I am that you are here —
Come upstairs with me —
Take off your bathing Frock —
You must be cold —
I have a warm Gown for you in stock —

Oh, Autumn, Do not feel doomed —
A long and burning Road you walked —
Did you leave Summer partly consumed —
Partly stored in the root cellar to keep —
The Maples — I must say —
They have sensed that you were on your Way —
Already they have begun to weep
In glorious blood-hues —

What's that sound? Who's there?
Oh, it's Winter knocking — cold air —
But I am occupied —
I will not be Pursued by frozen Winds —not yet.

Warmth will stay here still —
Even as begins the Chill.

Being a Female
Geraldine Connolly

after Pablo Neruda

I am sick of my hair and my lipstick,
my mascara and eyeliner.
so tired of my eyes, tired of my breasts
and my unspoken comments, tired of
my small footprints and the bandage over my mouth.

I am tired of men repeating my remarks,
pretending they were theirs.
I don't want to be a calf shut in a stall
waiting for slaughter,
a petroglyph smothered in a slab of granite.

It would be exciting to stab a shoe salesman
or paralyze a make-up artist.
It would be marvelous to ride an Arabian
stallion down Main Street,
while wearing a fringed jacket and cowboy hat,
opening my shirt for the world to see.

In the faint corners of photographs,
There I am, hidden in shadows,
stirring a pot, holding a small screaming baby
as birds fly out from the trees like desperadoes.

From now on I refuse to be a frail flower,
a petrified blossom, a rug that everyone
treads upon, lying still and miserable,
waiting for the next heel print.

I will grow smaller and smaller,
a hyphen, an afterthought,
a piece of lint fallen behind a pillow,

a woman who is no longer a female,
finally erased.

How Pleasant It Is, and Good
Charles A. Peek

after Philip Levine

What a pleasant thing it is
To have work you do, and also
Pleasant to have a place you go to do it.
Pleasant to have possessions about you
There, which you enjoy,
Which would be company enough
If they needed to be.
And how pleasant it is after a good day,
A day, say, when people have sought you
To do what it is you do,
And then to walk home to that other place.
Perhaps, it is later than usual,
But the sun is shining and the wind
Is still, the grass green, even through
Your dark glasses. That beautiful old tree
In the new people's yard is pleasant, too,
And so is Mr. Campbell's garden, grown
In his front yard so we can enjoy it.
And these are not, I think, common things
By any means. And maybe this once
They are yours, and good.

Muskrat
Don Johnson

after A. R. Ammons

The muskrat, flattened
on the slough
pushes upstream
toward the pool,
his wake defined
by a sun low
enough to shadow
ripples. A heron,
all wings, neck,
legs, glides
just above its head
aiming downstream.
On parallel planes
they pass
just as a trout rises,
scribing a ring
that grows to encircle
the muskrat.
Two hooded ducks
bob beyond its compass,
mergansers,
their crest fans
luminous
against the dark green
water, the brown stalks
of weeds on the bank,
the night already
scaling trees
on the far side
of the island.

The Last Stage
Carey Link

after Julia Darling

I try to read the colorless, asymmetrical hieroglyphics
in malignant, bilateral, inoperable . . .

My systemic silhouette sifts the sand in my hourglass house
through cycles of daylight and darkness.

He leads as we dance on a frayed tightrope.
He dares me to learn the routine as I go—
and jump over its holes with my eyes closed.

While I learn to breathe again.

How I Came to this World
Julene Tripp Weaver

after Gregory Pardlo

It was leap year, on a Thursday, I was born
        upstate New York, Borsch Belt small town.
To a family of farmers, where covered bridges crossed
        creeks. Twenty miles to the racetrack in
Monticello, our nearest city, where father worked
        for an air conditioning installation firm.
The Evergreens of the Catskills.
        A mother off seeking four-leaf clovers.
Born to arrowheads and quartz, to blueberry
        bushes in back fields. I ran to frogs
and salamanders across stone fences
        through wild woods, no eyes followed me.
It was during the cold war red scare, but I,
        a wild barn child was unaware. Daddy's little girl
I wore patent leather shoes at Easter and
        blue velvet at Christmas. The cameo necklace,
Mother gave me, fell into a stream. I was a wild thing
        from go, feeling the velocity of wind. The night
I came a fierce push. I was born clear white,
        pastel perfect skin, with spit-on Irish blood
and German ancestry I was told to never
        acknowledge by a direct line uncle. The year
I came, there was a storm brewing in the guts
        of women to have climaxes they'd never reached.
There was a surge to land on the moon. The
        Atom bomb was introduced from Britain. Born
in the year of the Dragon, I knew it would be rocky
        not a song in the rain, nor the cotton candy
fun world where mother resided.

Farmer's Daughter
Misty McCormick Chisum

after Elizabeth Bishop

Tired dry earth clods beneath my boots are Woman.
Exhausted fields without the will to produce
new life on demand, to yield to the machine
that crushes her mounds into tongue-tainting dust.
Crumbled in pieces at the start, she is ground
to moistness by blade, wheel, and probing fingers.

I watched her slow-slip through my father's fingers
each spring — single caress for the earth woman,
foreplay before the blade and the turning ground.
He took such pride in what his seed could produce,
what he could make of her, the dry Bootheel dust
with a touch and the pound of heavy machines.

A man's desire and the reaping of machine
love drew me to the fields and wrapped my fingers
around a hoe — my toes curled into the dust.
A girl with no desire yet to be a woman,
I admired the beauty she could produce
as I bent to pull weed roots from the moist ground.

I witnessed life spring from the womb of the ground
without considering the birth a machine
forced act — a plow as forceps ripping produce
from her earthen womb like a doctor's fingers
forcing life from reluctance — from a woman
who would trade moistness for the silence of dust.

The earth is a woman he told me as dust
poured through my hands and I believed as the ground
showed me the beauty of being a woman
and whispered to me of time before machines

when men gently caressed the seeds with fingers
into body, the harmony as produce.

A strong man will charm me and I will produce
children who will someday turn to the dry dust
that clung to my skin and ran through my fingers.
I will feel a kinship for my father's ground
when I bring forth life to the hum of machines.
I will know her then — I will be a woman.

I will lie still, fingers caressing the ground,
the meaning my father produced in the dust
clear in machine silence — the earth and woman.

Eggs
Lana Hechtman Ayers

after Stephen Dobyns

The gauzy morning sky over the ocean, over my little town, over the
coast range mountains presents like soft music to my eyes, to my
heart, perhaps Debussy's Clair de Lune, or Beethoven's restrained
Moonlight Sonata, more nocturne than aubade. I've never been a
morning person, sun a brash interloper to the landscape and to my
ruminative thoughts, my daze. I may be crazy, the only one who sees
the world prettier this way, in haze, inner glow showing through
while the sun's shaded, the perk of life emanating from within green
leaves, blue-green sea foamy with froth, gritty beach sand. Even the
oblique, distant hills radiate subdued gray haloes. Time feels slower,
kinder in this hushed daylight, no need to rush anywhere. I stare out
until the music ends with a crescendo of bright sun breaking through
marine layer. Time to turn to the day's work, the mundane to-dos of
those who must earn their keep this capitalist hamster-wheel daily life
requires. I once aspired to something other, something deeper than
consumer, and as a teenager, imagined myself becoming a vagabond
poet hitchhiking back-country paths. But I majored in Mathematics,
not literature, well aware how fond I was of indoor plumbing and
eating several times a day, not to mention a particular French roast of
coffee that cost a premium, and of which I imbibed way too much.
Some mornings my caffeinated heart threatened to thump its way out
of my chest. Once employed, I was testy with my joyless actuarial
co-workers who never questioned calculating human frailty statistics
to improve the insurance company's bottom line, lives only part of the
equation in so far as it meant avoiding costly payouts for injuries. It
was a soul-numbing job I couldn't wait to be done with. Occasionally
though, I think of that one supervisor who was more human than the
rest, dressed more casually, Polo shirts never button downs with ties,
his Fred Flintstone head, enormous jaw and nearly no neck, and a
laugh that bounced in and around all the cubicles on the west side of
the twenty-fourth floor. Always in good spirits whether your numbers
belied the corporate line, he wanted to know about my poetry. I was

a little in love with him for that, and maybe would have stayed in the job longer to see if we had any chemistry if he hadn't been married. I was lonely, having lost the only boyfriend I believed my soulmate. He could see into my dreams when we slept side by side, awake, verbalize my thoughts before I spoke them, so deeply did he know me. To be seen this way, intimately and intensely, to be known was so beyond what I believed love could ever be. But after a while he didn't want me, needed to date wilder women who would facilitate confronting his own demons in ways I could not. Our shared therapist told us we possessed diametrically opposed neuroses. No dose of medication I could take would change that. I'm not sure, exactly, when I got over that lover as the phrase goes. I suppose I realized a life with him would be about his tremendous ego, me catering to his needs and subverting my own passion to write. Not that being a writer fits the romantic notion I once carried in my head, creativity being such a mystery. I believed I could be a person of worth if my words carried the correct currency, coins of knowledge, dollars of stark originality. I hadn't the sense to know writing is not synonymous with fame for most. Though it wasn't really fame, I see now, that I ravenously craved, but respect, having so severely suffered its lack growing up. Dorothy Parker said something to the effect, if you have friends who want to become writers, the second best thing you can gift them is *Elements of Style*, the first, of course, is to shoot them while they're still happy. Who's ever happy? I used to consider suicide a lot, all the while I was writing. Coincidence or not, I don't know. Mostly, when young and foolish, I thought maybe I had a knack for storytelling, for poetry, and surely, anyone who read my work would know it. Then came reality—critique and comparison, the two fatal Cs. Once installed in the mind, they multiply unencumbered, a cancer of self-doubt. It's past time now, I should get on with this too sunny day, run errands, pick up mail, fetch groceries. I always think I'll get lucky, find there's no sold out sign along the three roadside egg stands. Living in a farm town, though mostly dairy cows, I feel nearly entitled to the just laid little ovals of glory. But I am always too late. Those human-sized birdhouses where the eggs are stored, pitched along Bayocean Road and Netarts Highway, function on the kind of trust that's all too rare in man's 21st century—take your dozen and stuff the correct cash in the wooden box, neither stealing money nor eggs, as less honest passersby may do. That kind of faith in humanity these days, when the world is falling apart more than usual, is hard. Killing the environment as we are, impermeable bigotry, senseless shootings, greed in every shade of ugly. And yet, leave it to the humble egg farmer to offer what he has too much of, and what he knows we all love, those orange, gooey yolks, scrambled, boiled, sunny side up, or combined in recipes, a natural alchemical magic, as necessary an ingredient as language is to connection, to story, to this poem I've been trying and mostly failing to relate to you. May the rains come soon, drown out this overage of sun, this overdone brightness. May I find the right words, crack them open, one by one, sticky, globular, elegant.

In the grease room's dark
Allen Braden

after Theodore Roethke

(somewhere above
the stacks of retreads and rings
of stockpiled air filters

and rough pine planks that sag
under cans of every kind of paint
failing to approximate a rainbow,

where the top shelf's a stash
of *Hustlers* and *Playboys*,
the chew roll of Copenhagen)

a single valentine from the drugstore
is hidden, with not a smudge
of grease or dirt on it.

Would it be hyperbole then
to say turpentine and thinner
perfume the air;

say the cobwebs
are like costume jewelry
accessorizing the beams and rafters;

their specks of dust,
tiny rhinestones
after last night's killing frost?

Even the dead flies
and drops of oil spilt from drums
glitter in the weak and dirty light.

This Poem Is for You, Reader

Linda Simone

after Walt Whitman

whom I will never see, never meet,
except across this inscribed proscenium.
Will you glean my grains
threshed across a life?
Lean like stalks of wheat
toward love
no matter what, no matter who,
hijabed woman,
white-masked klansman,
children hunted and hiding,
parent who adored
and failed you?

Under the scrim of night
set things right.
Carry your props—
people, birthplace, circumstances, century—
and build a tableau of sunlight streams
where sparrows glide,
where all is one
where you, I, we
enter Sanctuary.

On a Landscape Job You Pour New Wine into Old Skins

Peter Ludwin

after Robert Wrigley

Out of a fable framed with willow and fiery
sword the Garden of Eden scribes fashioned

a fall, a future uncoiling like wire, scarred
by thorn, thistle, toil and woe, a crimson arc

splashed across the sky: the angel of death.
But today, wrestling with ivy in an old man's

yard, you feel sweat break out along your brow
and think, *this* is paradise. This moist aroma

of decay from soil disturbed, the roots ripped
and rearranged that proclaim a common glory.

The strain of sinew, like the sound clippers
make as they sever multiple stems,

awakens the pores. With each clump
tossed in a plastic bucket you save yourself.

Again and again, the world. How is it
you are so blessed to turn toward your face

fingernails blackened with dirt? To struggle
with resistant vines? You stand to stretch

your back and a velvet-antlered buck appears.
Come, you say, let us break bread together.

From These Pancakes, Multitudes Eat
Ann Cefola

after Walt Whitman

The kitchen crowded: Someone rolls
a chapatti, folds and rolls; ladles ground maize,
tilts crepe pan. My hand signals *warm the syrup*.

Bedouin tribesman, Aztec princess, Parisian chef,
uncountable cooks, and me — measuring oats,
jostle bowls and flip dough until gold in heat:

Hummus-stuffed pitas brushed with olive oil.
Tortillas cradling green onion, pinto, corn.
Sucre-dusted crepes of berries ripe red.

How can my breakfast table fit this feast?
Before I answer, someone says grace.
We grow quiet. Eat.

After a Health Scare
Lynne Burnett

after Cecilia Woloch

Him I love, with hair like saltmeadow rush,
eyes that beach me on unexpected shores,
mouth of a wild and generous sea

Under whose spell children have flown
to the moon, from whose lips the secret
lives of teddy bears told

In whose hammock of shoulders my heart swings,
his moonlit back a white bench, buttocks smooth
as ancient boulders

In whose countries of hands I am born again,
whose tongue is both midwife and stirring
anthem

Him I love, whose ticklish feet like gold bricks bank
on never being touched, legs of a mustang,
rain in the wind

In whom has lived the grip, the gale, the gall
of a thing, who as the world turns
is my world turning

Upon whose sun-blessed chest I lay my head,
hear the hammering, thank again the small
gods at work in their chambers

Molting
Jeanie Sanders

after Anne Sexton

I dreamed there were snakes in my belly
alive and waiting to be born.
That any minute I would be
a mother to reptile flesh. Most nights
I dreamed the same wiggly dream
until my husband began to sleep
in the spare bedroom. I did so wish
to be a mother. To hold something
of myself in my newly mother arms.

For years I hoped and dreamed
but then bled away any life inside me.
Until the doctor told me your womb
must go or you could die. So with
enough tears to fill a minor ocean I said yes.

Afterward my husband moved back
into our bed. Some comfort but still
on very rare occasions I had those
snake dreams. But now the snakes were
unwilling to be born. Instead they began
to eat their way toward my mouth
and fill my voice.

The Use of Force
Jim LaVilla-Havelin

after William Carlos Williams

I wrote this story
        from my
            doctor life

about the struggle with
     a child
        fear
          and shame

I know in my hands
          in my
             feet

how much
      depends

        upon

          consent

American Sketches: On a Proposed Trip South
Carly Lynn Gates

after Donald Justice

Somewhere south
of Daytona
palm trees had
begun to appear
and wave their
fringed limbs at
the bus windows
to travelers who
would not stop
for warm sands
nor seaweeds that
crashed with the
surf just behind
the eyelids of
passengers who
were asleep with
the hum of wheels

America, Where Are You?
Carolyn Chatham

after Lawrence Ferlinghetti

I'm waiting for that hard rain Dylan prophesied.
I'm waiting for America to awaken from its stupor
and fulfil its promise.
I'm waiting for that eagle to fly off its dollar
and do something noble with its talons.

America, where are you?
Some of us are looking.

I'm waiting for love to conquer hate.
I'm waiting for the meek to stand up
and stop glorifying their cowardice.
I'm waiting for Jesus to un-nail himself
and come off that plaster cross
and unplug the television preachers.
I'm waiting for that sign that affirms
that all men, and women too, are finally
and truly equal.
And most of all, I'm waiting for our heroes
to stop killing and come home
to save us from ourselves.

America, where are you?
Some of us are looking.

I'm waiting for Lady Liberty
to douse her torch
and cease luring the poor
and downtrodden to our shore
just to send them away again.
I'm waiting for that hard rain Dylan prophesied.

America, where are you?
Some of us are looking.

I'm waiting for that crack in the Liberty Bell
to heal itself
and to finally knell,
to ring out the old and ring in the new.

America, where are you?
Some of us are looking.

The Angry Poem Circling Urban Grit All Night in Search of Tenderness

Ron Smith

after Phil Levine

A man who has never been
a boy and a woman
gray as Detroit
lean against the hard wall
of the empty hotel.
They are too tired
to read this poem.
The are too tired
to find a smudged place
to lie down and do it.
I could tell them that.

I could tell them to cross
the broken river
like the dead going home
and wait near the freeway
for some angels.
How much can it hurt?
I could give them each
a hankie and send them
to Barcelona
where nothing would change
but the smell
of their breaths:
salami.

But it's better here
near the slag heap's
yellow flame where
the rain won't quit.

I'll make her touch
his worn hand.
I'll make him stay up
all night over coffee
in that diner, telling
her all the bad facts
of his life.
I'll make her smoke,
look out the greasy window,
until she says,
You can have it.

He'll gasp, Am I gonna
make it? I'll take them
to where the road ends
at a pile of crankshafts.
They'll lie down
in a cheap room
in their crusted clothes,
and she'll say,
You can have it.
But they'll both fall asleep
and sleep like the dead,
their mouths open, filling
with the clouded light
of morning.

Lone Star
Philip Wedge

after William Stafford

The drive home is a routine, same turns,
same movement out of an expanding
city, across the river, past fields where
now the harvesters are still, the plows readying
ground, the red-tailed hawks sitting on poles
they will hunt from until just before spring.

The road we take has many turns, including
the next-to-last, where once when you were sleeping
your mother, who was caught napping too, clipped
a pole and brought the car to rest against
an old culvert of an abandoned road,
the kind of event a five-month-old would
rather sleep through than wake to dream about.

Why you know the corner, why this place registers
in your mind, we don't know, but there it is:
soybean fields plowed dark brown again, grass
trailing up to hills where horses, cows and new-built
neighbor houses wait, a place we come to
in the dark, ready to turn at a country corner
only different from the others by its out-of-place
streetlamp shining over a road-crew's sandpile.

Even in the dark, you know this spot, not yet
two and a half, travelling on a night
much like the one two years ago, same season
as well. We pass the forgotten curve, head
towards the street-light before gliding to our
tiny town, and your dreamy voice drifts up
to us from the car-seat in back: "Almost Home!"
reminding us to stay awake, to watch you grow
out of this dark, toward the promise of some other light.

The Roaring Life
M. L. Lyons

after Dylan Thomas

When I was a witchy girl, I beguiled
the boys with my moon-wide stares,
    teased their lips, their loins
    with a wash of milky thigh til
    they wriggled in their pews
when I kneeled at Sunday prayer.

    On every sultry Sabbath eve,
I favored one fasting lad to lick my fingers
    Clean of dimpled sweets and sup
    On the sight of my satiny breasts
    Til trembling, his locks and lips wet
    He curled in desire at my knees.
    Then he begged, he cried, he swore
His sweet soul to any horny-headed deed.

    When I was a witch of a woman
Though the black bearded preachers warned
    At the climax of every sermon
    To watch how the wanton adorn
    And only worship a lonely virgin
    Who stood in a corner and mourned.

    My Sabbaths were still salty and sweet
For I and the moon and the men we mingled
    and rolled like the waves on the shores.
    There I dipped in delight and
    my thighs how they shimmered
    In the dewy dusk of the morn
As the church bells toiled in the steeple
    To call them back to their fold.

For my hips, they swayed to a wilder rhythm
As they longed to reach pleasure's door.
Come Sunday, the deed was never revealed,
But my scent how it lingered in the incense
And my body how I lay in their prayers
Even as the priest thundered in his pulpit
And the church bells dangled in the air.

Now I witch the wild wide world
There's a rich reward for the roaring life
and my Sabbaths are always warm
For I became no Sunday wife
Chaste in a dovecoted room.
I whistle through the night in the cat black skies
And I sleep with whomever I please and
Pleasures still reside between my thighs
Just as fallen angels still have wings.

Mirror Fugue
Sally Ridgway

after Kathleen Graber

Once, as a young woman, I curled on a window sill in Chicago
anticipating the thrill of streets below. Now it's the charm of mirrors.

My friend's high-rise room of mirrors — above birds, Lake Michigan
    to sky.
Lost in tall windows, dwarfed by architectural drawings, mirrors of all

sizes, simple frames elongated or a triptych of tiny sepia rounds
in lacy wires. No matter how small — ever spacious and undefended.

Mirror as in *mirari: to wonder and smile.* Smile as in *whimsy: to
    wander with the eyes.* That's what I want — to enter the spell of
    the room.

"I don't look in them," she says. "Me, either," l lie, grabbing my bag
of tricks, paint my lips red, protruding; wrinkles recede, eyes darken,
    grow.

Thomas Cromwell said the worst of Savonarola's bonfire of the vani-
    ties
was losing the mirrors. Without them we can't tell ourselves from the
    beasts.

He didn't know that orcas, apes, whales and elephants pass the mirror
    test.
Best, though, is looking at them slant. The rug mirrored beside me

reveals its deco-mannered tulips, windmills and dragons indigo/green.
I see them new. The standing lamp bows down. Blinds become an
    escalator

angling out from a dark corner. An empty frame teases. A mirror

reflects
a window, its garden below. In the morning of lake stillness and sun-
    tipped

trees I rediscover my loveliness. And a man walks from the garden
into the mirror. The same man walking twice, both sides of me! Con-
    fusion

can be a spiritual state. This kaleidoscope light. Move and it can
    change,
recede to the primal mirror — a pool of water dark as a creek. A
    sycamore

quivers at its center. It is distortion, calling us to the details of a thing.

At Starvation Falls
T. R. Poulson

after Robert Bly

Those gusty Gorge winds start suddenly at the cloud line.
Trails only go so far.
The mountain biker leaves his cheating lover and drinks no more
    wine,
the daughter walks to Bridal Veil Falls and makes herself at home.
The widower unlocks his boat and catches three more fish.

And the bruised wife hikes Mount Defiance, but loves her husband
    once more.
The energy builds in the wind, and two windsurfers jump off swells in
    the barge lane.
It will not go away —
We all know them, the ones always flying, whose feet touch nothing,
    as though safe.

And the mother returns to Hole in the Wall Falls, where she made
    love with her son's father.
She searches for her beloved, but never sleeps alone.

As the water tumbles from peaks, the salmon go on swimming up-
    stream.
The boy gets out of high school, reads many more books,
and learns that (long ago) drifts of snow stopped two trains at Starva-
    tion Falls.
The men took out their shovels and skis, but nobody starved at all.

The toe of the brown boot pivots
at the edge —
The man in the bright t-shirt topples from the cliff.
No one knows why he chose that trail, or how he fell, or if he hiked
    alone.

Glee
Mary Horner

after Jack Keroauc

The loss of color
Leaves us with a shadow
Cast long and low
Over smooth fields
And crags of air that deepen
Toward the soul of the earth
In equal measure.

The air is uneven, heavier
On the side of the innocent.
Windows frame the view
Like a stage that never
Closes after everyone
Moves toward home.

I breathe in after you
Filled it with despair,
Allowing me the privilege
Of hearing you set the
Record straight for the
Third time in history.

The colors we see
Inside the message are
Blurred by particles of lies
that risk the lives of
Everyone you've never met.

Masked America
Connie Ann Kirk

after Walt Whitman

Governor closed the buildings down, the parks, the schools, the trains, the pubs, the local flower shop selling tulips for a dollar; the barber who stayed open behind the scenes anyway spitting germs into the hairs of a dozen unsuspecting patrons as he regaled them with stories of the latest he'd heard from Jim, the old ballplayer who's in on Wednesdays; Gov closed the diner that now serves breakfast as take-out on the curb, bagel and a coffee to go alongside you as you go to nowhere in particular besides just back home to where your wife and kids drive you crazy and the homeschooling, well, when were you ever good at homework, after all; the factory where brushes for brooms and hair without germs get made and the tiny kind of brushes mimes use to dab paint on sad faces, nowhere to go now, not one funny thing about it, not one thing to not say aloud to amuse a crowd that's not there; the libraries, the one thing upon which the un-accessed depend for news with no access at home; the trains overnight getting dis-infected,

the homeless population resurrected from slumber on subways to shelters out somewhere, anywhere else; the museums where people get art for their hearts to start, no more; the theaters where escape into cinema, music, drama has gone silent for those with too much entrapment around them; the churches where droplets of grace have dried for congregants at home who hold onto faith, regardless, worshipping via tied tubes. Governor asked all to wear masks, to not cough or sneeze virus into others. Where is the hero, behind which mask is he or she lurking, waiting for the call, waiting for the light; is it that guy with the US flag bandanna or that lady behind cream lace or that student wearing solid black, or the rebel defying wearing a mask at all, certainly not that person. Who will save us with a breakthrough; who is the masked crusader, cape flowing like red milk; where is the hero who will not only treat, feed, deliver, protect us in the everyday, as so many brave ones have and do, but where is the one, the one who will, smile concealed, talent lent, power generated, save us all, bring back

those glorious, free days of the mystery of breath,
in and out,
in and out,
free. clean. alive.

A Denver Dawn

Susan Swartwout

after Gerard Manley Hopkins

I saw this morning's red-tailed hawk riding a new wind,
Denver's dappled dawn reflected on his grudging back,
the stern claws underneath, clutching death,
guarding flesh fresh from the neon-drawn night before,
now streets parched of prey, prostate below him.
I walk these 6 a.m. mile-high boulevards,
reading safety in shapes of other women
swinging their strides, pocketbooks free at their sides. Perhaps
this proud pace embraces a dawning city of women. Imagine us:
unchaperoned yet secure in our own warm flesh.
Navigating shadows, a few men hurl themselves harried along
other sidewalks, brute beauties who awoke to a changeling
world. They mutter opinions in their fathers' voices, claw
sweatshirt hoods around furtive faces in this fecund currency
under heaven anew, a thousand assumptions aflight, a cold dawning.

The wonder of it: women sharing a darkling morning downtown,
gliding unfettered, unleashed from fear's bondage, turn to find
no one sinking, slinking their suspect steps behind.

Grief Like Sand
Christine Rhein

after Lisel Mueller

It sticks to us in grains,
in countless scratches.

It spills into our beds,
our rugs, as if wanting us
to drag it through the house.

It swirls its way
into closets, cupboards,
the hollows of our bowls.

We taste it in between
our teeth whenever
we talk, try to talk.

Its wild dunes grow
all around us. We climb
and crawl, slip and slip,
sinking deep.

We remember filling
childhood pails with it,
shaping castles,
how easy it was
to moat, to topple.

onceagain
John Aicher

after e e cummings

somebody stirring
and yawning like new
(perhaps it's just me
with old how about you)
wants to enjoy
our return to again.
let's leave us alone
to recover surprise
(we'll go see the ocean
caress the sunrise)
and gather forever
(it's where we began.)

479G
Amanda Giles

after Emily Dickinson

A Creature lying in repose
Was staring at the skies —
I might have passed him, if the clouds
Had occupied my gaze —

A Shroud of needles from a Pine
Were wreathed around his form —
The Wind began to lift the hair
Upon my neck and arms

He'd never tunnel farther down —
Through loam trails Underground
A venture from his Haven-hole
Turned him to statue–stunned

His paws were fixed aloft and splayed
For help from some High King —
I stooped to ascertain why Death
Had come to this small being

Then, leaning for a clearer view —
I bowed, most wistfully
Before an infant star-nosed Mole
In his Mortality

This Fellow's unplanned funeral
Attended but by one —
He slept right through his tiny wake
And I walked on–Alone

Rewriting Canto Five of Dante's Inferno: Crossing the Piazza at Midnight

Pellegrino A. D'Acierno

after Dante

Earlier in the day
the sky over the piazza
was rendered apocalyptic
by the dark shroud formed
by the furiously rotating
flocks of starlings

vertigo zoom . . . the effect of
the lacerated azure sky

The *bufera infernal* runs its course
it is the hour of duets

As the night empties out the piazza
the street musicians track the lingering lovers
with "Bye, Bye Blackbird"
and the fire-eater
spumes his last arc of flame

In the café,
the inside of the outside,
Francesca silently nurses her
slow Cuba Libre while Paolo,
Bogarting his last Lucky Strike,
does all the fast-talking

Then like fastidious pedants
they perform with their gazes
an exegesis of Canto Five of the *Inferno*
in the scholastic version of carpe noctem

she assumes the role of a Dantista
while he plays Henry Wadsworth Longfellow
defending the correctness of his translation:
"Kissed me upon the mouth all palpitating"
They perform together
in silence its correction:

"All trembling

      he kissed my mouth

           all trembling"

It is the foreplay
to a night of dangerous love
in which they enact
the profane implications of the
word "bocca"
and cross the piazza
blissfully

      [NOTTURNO:
      THE BOOK OF HOURS CARESSES]

The Wound
Mike Graves

after James Wright

There is this wound
Within and beneath my stomach
That no one will ever make naked:
A scar, a mouth,
Gash of stigmata.
When my manhood hardens,
I wish I had never been born.

Don Welch and Effective Poetry
Betty Kort

after Don Welch

Last night I went to a poetry reading.
At the end of this most enjoyable evening,
some joker got up and began trailing off into hyperbole
about a childhood classmate who ate Crayola Crayons.

Now I can guess that most in the audience
could identify with the taste of crayon,
drawing back, as they might, to somewhere
in the recesses of their minds.

I myself know, from having indulged
in a tidbit or two,
that there is no difference in taste
between the colors of burnt sienna
and periwinkle blue.

But the deluded poet talked of a girl
who chomped down multicolored crayons
like a mower devouring hay at peak season.

"Hyperbole!" I exclaimed. That girl's mother
would have put an end to such perversion,
stopping it dead.

I dismissed the issue,
ambled home to warm milk and cookies,
and then went to bed.

Yet, this morning I awoke with a strange sensation—
a waxiness in my mouth and crumbling stuff over, under,
really all around my tongue.

And sure enough, when I stretched open my eyes
in front of the medicine cabinet mirror,
there was no mistake:
magenta, turquoise and yellow-gold
were ground into my teeth.

Did I discover anything else
you certainly might ask?

Well . . . yes . . .
Crest toothpaste doesn't fight
Crayola Crayon multicolored wax!

Running Water
Stuart P. Radowitz

after Gary Snyder

High
in the mountains
a swallow

spirals
her wings
and curls away

above
a tumbling, sparkling
spring.

Nothing is static.

Low fields
thick with wheat
fall to the thresher

and crumble
beneath his tractor
tires.

The Poudre River runs
up canyon.

Geese call geese
and gather together
gray-backed,

and green-necked
and great
in wild number.

Iced water
runs fast
past

spiked reeds reel
up crystal clear,

white caps
crowning white air.

Gold
lingering
in the after-

noon light
glazes the Poudre
perfectly.

The water crackles.

Her lips ripe,
split logs wedged
across the water

we crossed.
Taking her hands
I taste the wild water

and swallow.
The dark lily opens
her heavens.

Hamlet of My Childhood
Ulf Kirchdorfer

after Charles Simic

A draft from a cold room
has Hamlet visit me in a sleep.
He is a curious bird, like a spoon
that is the monster of my childhood.

Outside the wind blows and calls
the name of Hamlet, while we
huddle in the cold of my squeaky bed.

Here for the Ride
David James

after Russell Edson

for Russell Edson and Maya Angelou

The poets die off,
their voices buried under grass or burned
into pebbles of dust. I guess that's everyone's fate,
a blessing and curse, a sadness and comfort.

A son or daughter, husband or wife, sprinkles you out of an urn
into the back fields, by a favorite river or lake,
along the first base line at the ballpark.

Maybe this is the meaning of every poem
ever written: breathe and live while you can;
let the years scrape off like bark
so you can find yourself at home,
satisfied and content, ready for the next journey
into God-knows-where-land.

My friend claims that every poem
is about sex, love or death and the fear or need
for them in our sorry lives. But poets can
write about caged birds or cows falling into rabbit holes,
about eating apes or a small child losing her voice for years.

The world carries us slowly into the future.
Sooner or later, we pay the toll.

We Talk of Cemetery Plots
Barbara Novack

after Mary Oliver

We talk of cemetery plots
ponder pre-planning
reality closer than we'd like
while a blind brain still dreams.
Which is the reality,
the truth in the moment, this
moment
not that one, the one that brackets
time
contains, compresses
heightens it into stone
carves it with etching-acid rain
tears maybe, but we won't see
or know, since
no one's left to tell our story
but the stone
or the cloud-fluff sunbeam-streaked
morning out the kitchen window
where birds peck the spring lawn seeds
and branches bubble with nascent leaves' green haze?
We talk of cemetery plots
ponder pre-planning
wipe condensation from our eyes
with an index finger
draw a smiley face on the hazed window pane
where we can, if we dare,
look out and see
tomorrow.

Happily We Sit
Cindy Frenkel

after Billy Collins

We sip wine, companionably
watch bees hover over
foxglove and larkspur while cats
curl in circles beneath ferns
cascading from terra cotta pots.
You're the most indecisive person I've ever known,
you admit. I instantly reply, *I'm not sure that's true!*
We laugh. You pinch a dead hydrangea head.
We lower our faces, take tipsy selfies
documenting our newly doubled chins.
Larkspur. Phlox. I sense scents:
Lavender stocks abloom.
Above ground you've spun word-worlds,
planted in soil among roots of elms.
Mirroring the ombré sky, pearl-white petals
of evening primrose open slowly, slowly close.

Tappin' on Life's Core
J. F. DeVoe

after Bob Dylan

Lover, just make my clothes disappear
We don't need them anymore
It's getting light, light enough to see and hear
Yes, I'm just tappin' on Life's core.

Tap. tap, tappin' on Life's floor
Tap, tap, tappin' on Life's core
Tap, tap, tappin'. . .

Lover, take my smile for real
We make three-time evermore
The sun's bright, bright enough to kneel
Yes, I'm really tappin' on Life's core . . .

Tap, tap, tappin on Life's floor
Tap, tap, tappin on Life's core
Tap, tap, tappin . . .

Lover, be there if I am lost
We can dance through any hallway door
The time's right, right beyond its temporal cost
Yes, I'm still tappin' on Life's core…

Tap, tap, tappin' on Life's floor
Tap, tap, tappin' on Life's core
Tap, tap, tappin'…for more.

Isosceles
Julie Allyn Johnson

after Billy Collins

Hubby has golf on —
some major minor —
as I look up from a bowl
of Cheerios to see Cameron
Tringale hit into the drink,
slow smile arcing the distance
between my ears,
the supreme pleasure
of recognition
that with just a few alterations
his surname approaches
geometric proportions.

This Be My Verse
Terrell Tebbetts

With a Wink and Nod to Philip Larkin

They lift you up, your mom and dad,
   They always mean to, and they do.
They grace you with the gifts they have
   And add some extra, just for you.

And they were lifted in their turn
   By folks in old-style hats and coats,
Who wrapped them warm on winter days,
   With woolen scarves around their throats.

Man hands nurture on to man,
   It rises like a coastal shelf.
So start out early as you can,
   And have a lot of kids yourself.

Part II: Tributes

In Spider Season
Kevin McIlvoy

to Tony Hoagland

H liked to write about evening parties on backyard lawns
where people spoke conversational poetry as naturally
as nightgowns slouching near shambling jeans.
    The leaves — lookit them — they won't finish falling.
      Spider season. So many tree webs — nothing hits the ground.
        Nothing. No thing. Noooo thing.
Little drunk are we, ugly drunkling?
    They sing at night.
      Sparrows?
Sparrows specially.

He liked to make his own conversational poetry and enjoy
his own self-aware expressions of magician's silk
that would float and fall over and off you instanteasily.
    "Could I have your smoke?" he asked a smoker.
    "Could I worm my way in?" he asked the lawn.
    "Are these stars banksias? Is this microphone on?"
    He asked, "Must you with hot irons burn out mine eyes?
    These eyes that never did nor never shall so much as
    frown on thee?" He answered himself, "I will."

Well that was H for you,
a small person, his bed-hair tonsure
fainter after illness, big hands
bigger than ever before,
his crackling laughter coming still
from far away but now farther.
H would not give stinkeye
without stank on it,
not grace without gristle.
He was indelicate

with delicates.
He had good memory ears
for the failed rockets of song trailing
from poorly made launching pads.
Vaulted
he vaulted.
Of what H bit
he had a good bite.
Enjoined
he joined.

H was hymnary.

On this particular night of spider season, one of the party crashers
flicked a lit butt up where a web caught and swung and tricked
light upon the strands of spiderscript to the outermost margins.
        Her older sister hit her with The Mother Stick.
  They called it that?
      And that shit hurts like a high note.
    Like a docked tail.
      Like a like a like a —
What?

Grinding himself like a pestle
into the grass near Mr. B, Mr. H asked,
    "Space for another silence here, my brother?
    "Why knot-socks slobber-trails Rumiscopes?
    "I have been meaning to ask you, Why verbs?"

    "B, oh B," he asked, "tell me what bread said
    at the funeral of wine, of olive oil, of bread.
    Why so hungrily afraid of hungering?"

And the crasher strafed the lowest black lace
with his fingertips, collapsing the incomprehighest nests
and the suspended heaven-nestlings, and said, Next time
I guess you'll invite me, bitch, and punched the hostess

who punched back hard, and harder yet,
dropping the whole ass of the asshole down,
saying to him, You're invited for more anytime.

Mr. H, reconcilable to enemy-friends of friends
who inhabited the same snares as he, the same
perplexing era of perpetuating errors,
offered his hand to help the capsized man
rise, to move him into his own and Mr. B's open
wings, to lift him in only three whole notes of time
past the gloss of our longdesiring faces and
our night-singing companionship, into our collapsing
sanctuary of most almost almost joyful union,
    said, "Be embraced, Millions!
    This kiss to all the world!"

What I Would Have Said
to Seamus Heaney
Robert Hamblin

to Seamus Heaney

I'm older than you,
if only by a year,
but too old to have been standing here,
like a teenaged, awe-struck groupie,
for the past two hours,
hoping somehow to gain entrance
to your sold-out reading
at the National Portrait Gallery.

But we have more in common
than our age
and our love of poetry.
I too am a farmboy
who remembers what it's like
to dig and plant and harvest,
and I too grew up in a land torn
by hatred and violence and killing,
and I too listened to radio voices
from far away,
promising escape,
and I too now live in exile
from my past.
And, like you,
though not nearly as well,
I write about it all.

When I read your poems
I remember cotton fields,
not potato drills,
the conflict of races,
not religions,

radio voices from Chicago,
not Stockholm,
escape from the American South,
not Northern Ireland.

Very different worlds,
yet very much the same.
And when I read of yours,
I learn of mine,
and myself.

I just wanted to say thanks.

Storm at Cedarmere
Joseph Stanton

to William Cullen Bryant

The sound swells and turns above Bryant's
autumnal home as rising winds flail
the trees, and pale-white mists shroud
upland steeps, turning gloom inside out,

hollowing clouds of bright such as Tom Cole
could color at the heights of Kaaterskill.
One bay window finds Bryant's pond a cold
bright stone of light in hands held out,

an offering to the slanting dark of rains
that won't end soon. The other window sees
the harbor wanting to keep on gleaming
beyond all drumbeat melancholias,

over full with remaining alive,
giving Bryant delicate redeemings —
sweet, dangerous dreams of almost seaward —
held to his long island's vastness of Sound.

Dead Letter to Richard Hugo
Todd Davis

An abandoned pickup
rusts near a trailer
whose roof has caved in.

Along the valley floor
wood smoke loiters
and won't move on.

My friend's wife says
he needs to get a job
so he heads to the reservoir
and catches three trout.

There's a *For-Sale* sign
in front of the church. High up
still some stained glass, but
all the pews in the sanctuary
remain empty.

Dirt roads map everything
in squares before dead-ending
at the base of mountains.

The TV antenna
that peaks our roof
is a homily to the lack
of our ambition.

Although it's late
in the year, I dream
of a yellow-rumped warbler
singing outside the window.

Although it's late
in the year, I dream
of a yellow-rumped warbler
singing outside the window.

When I rise to look,
wind whistles
through a small bird's
skeleton.

On the Bank
Sarah Dickenson Snyder

to Lucille Clifton

It took an hour
to memorize the lines,
ending with sail

through this to that —
learning a prayer,
following a tide

that pulls a boat into a river
that widens to an estuary,
and out to the Chesapeake Bay.

It breathes us in, enters skin —
becoming a worded shield,
every rib shouldering

the horizon —
how words can be inhaled,
granular, travel with blood and stay.

I look out at the white-tipped sea,
taste the limestone air —
many lives in any one life

opening silently
in the wind —
everywhere a passage.

Over in That Corner, the Puppets
Jack Ridl

to Naomi Shihab Nye

Even when the weather changes,
remember to pet the dog, make
the cat purr, watch whatever

comes to the window. If you
stand there long enough,
someone will come by,

a stranger perhaps, one who
could be more, but needs
to keep walking. Hello

is likely all you can say.

Autumn Walk at Beechwood Farms
Judith Sanders

to Sharon McDermott and Christine Benner Dixon

You said, Name the world.
So I said, I call this a spangle tree.
How about, you said, a rose-hued spangle tree.
That's beautiful, I said.
Let's name the world together.
No, you do it, you said. What's this?
And held up a leaf. Red, three fingers.
Red mitten leaf, I said.
And that? Golden grain. Moptop grass.
Chewberry bush. A donglehopper.

How about this feeling? I said.
Can you name it?
Can you name this sunlit chill,
the meadow brown and gold,
the crunch and crackle
of leaves we shuffle through,
old friends rarely together?

Can you name how we remember
being here with sons now grown,
tossing pebbles in the water?
Here with that botanist
who won your heart
by naming every plant,
even the water weeds?

What do you call it,
what would he call it,
when we share tea on a bench
and homemade bread with apple butter?

When the trail is closed because
deer are being hunted
with bow and arrow?

Name the leaves dying around us,
bees probing skeletons of flowers,
deer pierced nearby.

Name slipping on wet leaves.
Name how I catch you.
Name me saying,
lean on my arm.
Name me not saying,
You should wear better shoes.

Name how the plants are beautiful in old age,
like our mothers, hair white as milkweed,
skin speckled with brown seeds.
Name how we cocooned
in their leaves.
How their stalks bent yet held
when we flew away.

Name it, name it all,
using only one word.
A word you search for.
A word you build
out of leaves and air.
Out of memories and forgetting.
Out of together and apart.

Come next November
will we remember this
view of bare branches
cascading below us
if we cannot now
find its name?

So name it, you said.
Name it with words
more beautiful
than the real names.

Elegy
Timothy Gauss

to Rainer Maria Rilke

A room echoes breathless
foreign to the soft caress
these walls provide

Let them crumble —
These ancient things
For the wind whispers
Disciplined and deliberate
Purposeful and boundless

Hidden in the empty spots
Between dust-kicked footsteps
Traversed roads untouched
Marred in resonance
grown, silently and earnestly
sculpted with precision and
undisturbed by violent gaze
in its quietest hour

Digging Lorca
James Penha

to Federico Garcia Lorca

Do soggy bones matter
more than Bernarda's broken
cane or New York
tenements or a perfect pair of olives
in hand? For if we hold, Federico,
your delicate fingers, trace the lines
of your lips with our fingers,
and hear your inspiration
even now, we have no need
for the palpable
to imagine you.

Desaparecidos reminds me more
of the next innocents
to die wordlessly
in a ditch.

Sonnet for Gertrude Stein
Sandy Feinstein

You wouldn't name a thing, for what is
isn't the point nouns make, impersonating
a rose won't smell rose or prick by touch
and leave blood no one wants to see

unless it's three spots of beauty,
Snow White, tautology of adjectives
that must be kissed awake to end adverbially
ever after, which omits the noun

I keep thinking about, after what
has gone before, mother, father
death, witches, apples, mirrors

after, what's to follow can't be named
despite the grammar of expectation
left just like that dangling finality.

You Do Not Have to Be Good
Carolyn Martin

to Mary Oliver

Ain't that a kick in the head!
After all the bunk about straights and narrows,
wrongs and rights, confessionals
where venial sins are laughable,
it's come down to this: we've been duped.
Friday fish, forty fasting days, crownings
in the Mary month of May; rosaries,
callused knees, indulgences that smudge
our sins: they don't add up to good.
Neither do tidy rooms, top grades in school,
nor mandatory modesty.

So let's delete the snake behind the apple tree
and every bite of stale theology.
Let's resurrect original wildness
and ramble through valleys scratched and scarred,
down unquiet streams, across raging fields
of blooms disguised as weeds.
Let's celebrate every fleshy flaw,
each mistaken thought that turns out true.
Let's race wild geese to the nearest star,
cheering on imperfect
nakedness with disheveled glee.

My American Prayer
David Cravens

> "James James
> Morrison Morrison
> (Commonly known as Jim)
> Told his
> Other relations
> Not to go blaming him"
>   — A.A. Milne, "Disobedience"

I was born in '71 — and by '79
I was looking in a mirror
after my father'd told me
he and my mom were divorcing

I felt the world crumble
like I'd been kicked in the stomach —
something I'd not before felt

years later
I'd picked up a book and read . . .

I think of myself as a sensitive
intelligent human being
but with the soul of a clown
that always forces me to blow it
at the most crucial moments

I still remember the words
as it's pretty well what I've become

& when I do these things
it feels like looking in that mirror again

you'd died in '71

but not all of us have grace
to exit softly in a warm tub

some of us bear our crosses
much longer

& thus I always hope
some of that old shaman
blew into me at your death

Shining Star
Dee Allen

to Amiri Baraka

I don't have too much
Time just sitting around counting stars.
I have to be in another
Part of town to accomplish that.

Alone, hiking around a dark
Bernal Hill with a flashlight,
I can see the stars above much
Better than I could in the Mission's
Drastic urban change below.

One shining star
Is missing from the ebony sky.
The hole it left is untraceable.
I've followed that star's
Brilliant shine for over twenty years.

Caught by its halogen-like luminence,
That star inspired me to craft
Poems that kill, wrestle cops in alleys,
Make me *feel and be me, shake off* to the
Best of my ability *madness and dead skull* songs,
Transform my home-spun writing into implements
That *splinter fire*, encourage me to *keep keep*
Throwing hard, keep on punching never
Let mine enemies *dodge* once,
Use my scrawled verses in daily struggle
That transcends class, as *my beautiful*
People with African eyes, nose and arms
Have for centuries, *wanting sun* aplenty
In a land where *heathens think*
Fascism is civilisation and *Luxury* is everyday

Comfortable ignorance.

In the slums, projects and blue collar suburbs,
There's always *a railroad made of* hella
Human bones — Black ivory, Black ivory, Black ivory —
When this situation worsens, *lovers & warriors*
And their sons should *unite* and come out
Fighting its conditions, even when the devil
With the blue uniform & badge shows up in a hot
Harlem minute — *IT'S NATION TIME!*
IT'S NATION TIME! IT'S NATION TIME!

One shining star
Is missing from the ebony sky.
The hole it left is untraceable.
That star disappeared, joining
Shining stars of the past in the endless void,
A parallel sky of sorts.
Like others that came before, that star unique

Newark street kid
Beatnik
Kawaida*
Communist
Not anti-Semitic
Anti-Zionist

More spirit than ghost
Born Everett Leroi Jones
Renamed Blessed Prince

Inspired me to pick up the pen
And fill notebooks with
Words that still move the people.

W: Martin Luhter King Birthday 2014
[For Amiri Baraka — 1934-2014.]
*SWAHILI: "Tradition". Afrocentric thought.

Questions
Nicholas Fargnoli

to Gerard Manley Hopkins

Your deep feelings for the natural world
    for its beauty
The passionate sensitivity
    you named instress
Discerned divinity
    sparked reflective insight
In a poetic imagination
    more theological
Than the romantic impulse
    from a vernal wood.

But your voice among others
    before and after
Was felled
    like those poplars
Lining the Thames along your walk
    and casting dancing shadows
To be seen no more
    on rippling current or rolling swells;
The riffling wind too
    is stilled
To be heard no more
    in swaying leaves and bouncing branches.

Is nature *never spent*
    . . . or is it?
Does hope have *mourning on*
    . . . or not?

Jack of No Grades

D. R. James

to Jack Ridl

Apt to wink at plans, languorous, aloft,
he forgoes mottos of the muscular,
maneuvers like a feather, and nearly
flies. Tough as a monk among his toys, and
boyish on trembling knees buttered by the
enchanted oil of home and the lingering
tinge of its contentment, there he bums, basks,
his whittling curling off whistling lines, lissome
lyrics weeding out unwarranted words.
Prof. Ridl weans his poets one-by-one.

Seer
Sheri Vandermolen

to Kamala Das

You are the ruby-eyed dragonfly
that alights amidst the dewdrops
collecting, in the cool of morning,
on a fresh lotus bloom.
You settle in meditative solace,
holding asana as you awaken
to the slow-growing words
springing from silence deep within.
Dawn exposes raw impulse,
and you take unhurried flight —
a crimson distortion of stillness
that was yours, yours alone.

Letter from an Old Poet
Anne Harding Woodworth

to Hayden Carruth

How kind you are —

> He doesn't really know if I am kind.
> He only knows I wrote to him
> about his book of letters to a dying friend —

to take the trouble to write to me.

> If anyone understands the trouble it takes to write a letter,
> it is he. Years ago he wrote one after another,
> confessed and shared his worries
> with someone he knew well and loved.
> I was writing to a person I didn't know at all.
> Short of dead, was he in possession of his faculties? —
> so obsessed his words seemed to be with his decline.
> I didn't know.

I went to school at UNC
and I know western Carolina
pretty well.

> I do, too. Pretty well, pretty well. Western North Carolina,
> filled with old people and young families.
> The guys at the Quick Stop drink Mountain Dew
> with a smoke before they go to work.
> They drive pickups with decals of big Dale Earnhardt No. 3's,
> rimmed in mourning black.
> Their bumper stickers say, "He lives."

But of course NASCAR was far in the future
in those days. I have never had the good fortune
to see a NASCAR race, except on television.

Me neither. But I've walked the Daytona track
when it was wet and they were desperate
to get it dry and vans drove round and round
heating it into evaporation.

On the other hand, I must confess
that my first love in auto sport
was small European sports cars,
and my preference as a spectator
is for Formula 1 machines.
I used to live near the Lime Rock track in Connecticut –

Skip Barber once asked me out —

but I was always a poor poet,
too poor to participate in a gentlemen's sport.

I told Skip I couldn't go. I was having dinner
with a friend of my mother's. He didn't believe me.
But he didn't say he didn't believe me.

If I could I would go to watch
races at Lime Rock or the Glen —

If I could, I would go watch races at Bristol —

but I am now too old and encumbered
by apparatus to go traveling.

Apparatus. What a lovely Latin word.
It could be so many things:
a walker, a wheelchair, oxygen, a flask.

As for driving I used to be
a pretty good amateur —

pretty good, pretty good

— but I would rather drive a Lamborghini
than a modified stock car any day.

I will buy him a Lamborghini.

I hope you enjoy the new season.

The new season is here in western Carolina.
It probably hasn't arrived in his North Country yet.
New season, the unknown.
It might bring pain. Apparatus, maybe.
No. 8 may die in a crash like his daddy,
all moisture might evaporate from the earth.
There will be rememberings galore,
comfort communicated to the dying.

For Emily
Geraldine Connolly

to Emily Dickinson

she listened in the hall
seldom crossed thresholds

baked dark cakes
with spirit-soaked raisins

dug with a trowel
at the edge of deep woods

dropped to her knees
to examine a caterpillar

rinsed windows with vinegar

while inside
intrigue twirled and spun

she loved
interruptions

which nothing could silence
or calm or cool

Losing Spenser in the Notes I Took in Class
Charles A. Peek

to Edmund Spenser

A gentle knight came pricking cross the plain
A perfect gentle knight came pricking quickly cross
Par Fit
A – sound – 3 – ag (1)-gra (2)-vat (3)- ing
Gentle — major etymological problem
Knight — knicked knight — nicked night — problem of dehistoriciz-
    ing
Gentle Knight—major oxymoron
Came – oops
Came pricking – double oops
Pricing — hidden word, economy, the fief
Cross — probably nothing
The — ah, Hemingway —"the" instead of "a"
Plain — could be geography (but sounds like geometry)
Not Spencer (with a "c")
Note includes: "Read the whole thing"
Must mean the sentence
Not the Faerie Queen.

Letter to Longley from the River House
Don Johnson

to Michael Longley

You were last here two dogs ago, Michael.
I've kept the photograph you sent of you
and Lani, the black Lab, on the deck
of the house on Nantucket Road. Another
life, another wife. Now I live by a clear,
cold river, filled with trout. Even the new dog
is four years old, a keen reminder
of your long absence.

The new house is old,
originally built when Washington
was president, and lived in through two hundred
hard years. I think of you each spring when
the tiller turns up broken dishes
in the garden plot. I know, the quilting
pattern of *Broken Dishes* only represents
the thick, blue-on-white fragments I puzzle
over, returning the mended cups and plates
to the hands that swept them from the dirt floors
out to the chicken yard or lazy bed
where they burrowed their way down in time.
But I can lose myself on the bare furrows
as you risked disappearance in the lushness
of your White Garden, coming back only
when the tiller coughs, or the spasm
in my left foot shouts, "Move on,"
to the next rock to lever out, or the one
piece of patterned fabric, a tomato tie,
left in the aftermath of last year's harvest.

Come back. I can't promise
you a hula in the living room

(other wife) but the guitar's in tune,
and I've saved a cantle from the antique
china. I could catalogue the things
you'd find delight in here, the way you named
"all the wild flowers of the Burren"
in my favorite poem, but birds and otters
are enough. And the new dog, Kona,
will prance and pirouette in greeting
when your lovely self comes through the door.

My Time
Carey Link

to Walt Whitman

. . . if you want me again look for me under your boot soles —

My time is growing russet.

Dress me in every color.

Sing me a song
of Four O' Clock Twilight
when sky melts
a tapestry
orange, rose indigo…
into a silver glitter —
I've met thousands of these.

Let me smell the hair
of a newborn baby.

Feel my tributaries
of blue —
each a beginning.

Warm me with the memories
you whisper.

Let me swaddle you in return.

Reflection After Reading Jane Kenyon
Julene Tripp Weaver

At the farm, it is a calm and simple world
disarming with its easy joys —
a daily walk with a dog companion,
trees and streams, each change
of season affects their eye.

It is a quiet pleasing place
with no TV, nor radio,
one grand grandfather clock.
Dinner parties are the exception.
Jane and Donald travel away
but always return, eager visitors
are scheduled with care.

But in this quiet resting place
beats all of life's travails
for no one can escape life's grit
that rubs us into age, illness, death.
There is no hustle bustle here,
peace fills long lounging days.

It slows one down to enter
this rural New England
Methodist, God faring land,
where people wait for loved ones
to return. It is a place
where a marriage lasts
until its dying day.

A sigh, a meager attempt to exhale —
left by the dispossessed lingers
like the trash they leave behind —
 a reminder of civilization,

the larger world outside.

Except, of course, for the poets —
Keats on his deathbed tiptoes around
gives his artistic inspiration. Russian
words are heavy, too, with Anna
Akhmatova's invocation.

Dancing on the Dead
Misty McCormick Chisum

to Sylvia Plath and Anne Sexton

When we were children
we danced together in the dust
with rock-hardened feet,
performing summertime séances
in the dirt road between our trailers.

We remembered the stone-faced
preacher speaking of dust
over the gaping mouth of grandma's grave.
You whispered to me of worms and open bird beaks —
how she had been transformed
into food for a starving world.

Dust to dust meant something different
to us —
when we realized that the dead
could rise again into air
if we twirled fast enough,
danced long enough.

The dead settled over us
and we giggled
at their gritty embrace
until we collapsed in a dizzy heap,
a pile of gangly legs and scrawny arms.

We climbed into our baths
at night and watched our mothers
try to scrub us clean,
to wash death away. We lacked
the words to tell them
that it would settle over us again,

that we would stir it into the air
so we could grind the grit
between our teeth.

We couldn't have known then
how you would like the taste
and the texture of it on your tongue —
how you would hunger
for it until your craving
left me here to dance this life
down solo with the dust
that is you stinging my eyes.

A Simple Truth
Lana Hechtman Ayers

to Philip Levine

I imagine Philip Levine time-
shifting in Trafalmadorian
fashion to 1936 where
he is an angel-on-the-shoulder
weeping as Lorca is tortured, then
murdered; to Fresno State his first year
teaching where on a lunch break he sits
with a student reciting Roethke;
to one April in Detroit, the mud
Biblical, men milling, cued up
for news of work that never arrives;
back to the mills, haunted as the men's
eyes who labored there, understanding
one human being is everyone.

And how many more lives than the six
million hearts stopped by Hitler does he
daily visit with his words? Grass, boats
dust, wind, the darkening skies, two sons,
a brother, the loves declared, unnamed
desires that were answered not by
their aims, but by the simple truths, small
red potatoes, melting butter, salt.

The book is open to the first page
yesterday. Tomorrow is always
the fourteenth of February. And
today it is 1941
five minutes to 8 AM, sweet Phil,
Billy Pilgrim, this day never ends.

Yes, oh yes, it is enough to say

what you can, the gift of transcribing
ordinary suffering into
extraordinary joy, your name
hangs in the brilliant morning air, a
feather, eyelid of a magpie, closed.

Sweethearts
Allen Braden

to James Dickey

One Friday late at night they grope their way
through the pale statuary and fallen leaves

for a hollow to lie in where they fit perfectly
the way their perfect bodies fit one another.

It seems quite natural that he is the star
this season and she the head cheerleader.

Once or twice she recalls something else
unforgettable she wants to say but does not.

They touch as if to say, *Don't ever forget this*,
are young enough to wring love from elegy

with the vertigo of their longing, the rush
of uncovering and pushing flesh against flesh.

One tiny act is all it takes to bury themselves
in some small excuse for somewhere else,

anywhere but right here where his ambitions
will be planed down on the graveyard shift

and hers will be spent waiting on tables
with trays of coffee, hot cakes and syrup.

Emily's Dress

Linda Simone

to Emily Dickinson

Her tidy bright package
I am single fascicle that caressed
tiny bird-boned frame.

At pine desk
overlooking King Street
words flowed

through
my covered-button sleeve
page after page.

Oh, never-to-be bride,
pure light
white aura from my folds

another might have been
buried in my cloth
but here I stand

displayed in this house
for all to pray:
Hail Emily, full of dashes and off-rhyme

the line breaks with thee.

Remembering Theodore Roethke after a Return to the University of Washington
Peter Ludwin

— What's madness but nobility of soul at odds with circumstance?

A bear of a man, you were. A frown fixed
   as the bark of a Douglas fir grooved your face.
A scowl that signaled like a boil a gear internal
   was amiss even as it belied the cadences

that propelled your words like driftwood.
   The reigning god of all who strove
to hallow language, in life you could whine,
   you could find fault. In the poems, never.

We didn't know the story: electric shock, the wild
   bi-polar rides you took at your amusement park
where water flowed uphill, then fled in ways
   no one could predict. But even if we had known

we wouldn't have cared. For us it was about rain
   that misted stanza, image, line. Soaked
the supple riot of bamboo, compost dizzied
   into floral displays whose fragrances

and scents drove those devoid of nectar
   into their own dry soil to plumb
a vein or seam. If lucky, strike the core.
   From the Quad I stroll to the greenhouse

on lower campus where vines ascend in a humid,
   clammy tangle. This was always my link
to your world: vegetation rank and reaching,
   loam rich with rot. My hands, too, had pillaged
soil and root, labored under baskets draped

in heliotrope and fuchsia flounce, encircled
pots molded green. Known the yoke of tactile,
  the drill imposed by hoe and trowel and rake.

In *The Lost Son* I found the same aromas I'd inhaled
  doing that work: the odor of earthy desecration,
of geraniums on a bench. Scanning its lines,
  I absorbed wonder braided with wound.

This spring, digging up ferns to plant peonies,
  I observe buds strain to open, to ignite
the world. As with poems sometimes, I stake
  them to keep them upright in the wind.

Dialing the Dead at 3 A.M.
Ann Cefola

to Thomas Lux

Poke index to punch — digit after digit, disbelief: *this line has been
disconnected.* Play reel-to-reel conversation that spins; rewind,
play again.

Fast forward to what I'd share: *My mother starved herself; I got As in
slow math.*
You can never know a person, a guru declares. We can only see street
light

spill through blinds and try to identify mirror, bureau, chair in mono-
chromatic dark.
Some, outside, can name stars and pull down their fire to ignite sleep-
less hearts.

Long ago, the operator could cut the line if you'd made joke calls,
and phone
your mother to tell her why. I'd like to ask her to break into the busy
line of one

who must still craft comets and campfires somewhere—the heat and
spark
they still give — operator, if you're listening — the real art was how
he lived.

Jane Kenyon Lives Again
Lynne Burnett

to Jane Kenyon

as an abstract painter in my neighbourhood,
"Yielding to Transience" the theme of her
current exhibition, according to the pamphlet.
It's that simple, the only life we have we'll lose
in a neon nose dive or the drift of gradual surrender.

My Jane, who briefly entered and briefly spoke
in poems — having it out with melancholy —
said *Let evening come* and it did, under cover
of leukemia, far too soon. Wish it were otherwise.
A moody harvest, those notes from the other side.

Now there'll be a conflux of Janes when I see
one's art, read the other's poem. A conjuration —
open sesame into the chambers of two hearts.
The amazing echoes, bone's signature marrow
waving its wand again, sweet Om on the tongue.

To One Shortly To Die

Jeanie Sanders

to Walt Whitman

He carried his poems into old age on pieces
of paper so that when he was dying those words
were his blanket keeping him warm with
their syllables and sounds.

Sometimes he was helped from bed to his front porch
where sunlight glazed his eyes with a rim of crimson.
A color that haunted his sleep as he dreamed
of the aftermath of battles were fields of the dead and
dying were flung over the Earth like trash.

There were waking dreams on that porch too.
Waking dreams of soldiers he remembered tending
with care as he held a cup of water to parched lips
or listened to rambled stories of war and better times.
Often he wrote letters home for those he carried in his heart.
Those slow breath of words each wounded soldier spoke,
so different and yet so alike.

Phil's Cities
Jim LaVilla-Havelin

to Philip Levine

with characters —
brothers,
workers,
drunks and
others
and they
all have
names
the characters
and the cities —
the streets, the bars,
the factories,
corners where
they waited
for the bus

named
specific
real

because
he holds them
close

The Writer's Wife
Carly Lynn Gates

after reading Galway Kinnell's "The Call Across the Valley of Not Knowing"

For years I have imagined that red house, sinking
into the dark earth, and I've placed her there,

Kinnell's first wife, her belly swollen with life.
She reads for the first time his poem about lying together,

two mismatched halfnesses, as her husband dreamed
of another woman, his true half, still moist with youth.

How must she have felt, their second child thrashing
inside of her—did she already agree with him

that her happiness lay in sleep? In dreaming
of lying in some other room, of a less fickle moon?

She must have once gladly held the blossom
of his empty heart, kissed the wound of his mouth

full of poetry, full of nightmares, but how long
could she last when he sliced open the scab

each time the flesh tried to heal, viewed happiness
as blindness already fat and soured by heaven?

How long could anyone? My husband's patience wanes.
I watch for the glowing ember of his cigarette

as he paces outside, surprised each time it reappears.
We cannot blame Aristophanes, Kinnell, only ourselves.

No moon can brighten our nightmares:

writers who sink with our houses, spouses who escape outside.

Kinnell's wife tears out the root of her heart, buries
it for earthworms. This darkness closes like a fist.

That's No Way to Say Goodbye
Carolyn Chatham

to Leonard Cohen

Leonard Cohen has died.
Dirty thing to do to us, Leonard,
to exit like that.
No heads up,
No warning.
No, "Hey, Poets,
I'm about ready to leave now."
Nada.
Not a nod or a flick of the pen or hand
as far as we can tell.

Gone, that small thin giant whose lines
nested in our hearts,
Whose lyrics came home with us
to our empty houses
and apartments,
Who fell in love the same as we
and "lived and loved and lived
and lost again."
Who kept us company
on park benches
and cheap rented rooms
and patio marathon readings.

I raised my daughters on your pain.
Your "tower of songs" their wellspring.
Your story of Isaac the only one they knew.
We were there, Leonard,
down by the river.
We ate those oranges too
and that dark chocolate
melted in our minds

the same as yours.

Then one day
We see the headline:
"Leonard Cohen has died."

How many poets wrote to tell you, Leonard,
Hey, Lenny,
"That's no way to say Goodbye?"

We should have written sooner.

E.P. in the Garden
Ron Smith

homage to Ezra Pound & Hilda Doolittle (H.D.)

Up the big maple
into my brother's crow's nest,
        the house hidden by leafy branches . . .

Beyond the hedge occasional cart, carriage,
                every half hour, a rattling tram
jolting past . . . He must not miss
        the last car, the train to Wyncote.
        "There's another
in half an hour." "Ah, Dryad," he says . . .
        We sway
                with the wind, with the clouds . . .

Finally, finally, we slide, slip through the branches, leap
        together to the ground, the solid ground.
    "No," I say, "no," drawing back, a girl
        of my time and place.
                "I'll run ahead and stop
        the trolley, quick, get your books, whatever
                you left in the hall." "I'll get them next time,"
        he says. "Run," I say, "run." He just
                catches it, nearly falling, the trolley, swaying . . .

Now, I face them in the house,
                Father winding the clock, Mother
    saying, "Where were you?
                Didn't you hear me calling?
        Where is Ezra Pound?"
        "Gone." "Books? Hat?" "He'll get them next time."

[Author's note: This piece is drawn primarily from H.D.'s End to Torment, New York: New Directions, 1979]

Deaf and Blind
Philip Wedge

to Jack and Ruth Clemo

He spreads his palm; her fingers spell the words
as readers recite poems he cannot hear.
His lips move to the print upon a page
remembered before sightlessness arrived,
or spelled out braille points from more recent years.
She knows he knows the poems that are read
and taps beginnings, the lines that move her.
He grips his leg as if in sudden fear
That we are watching them communicate,
but his mind goes on reciting when she
stops; the words and meanings are for him, one.

Elegy for Eavan

M. L. Lyons

to Eavan Boland

Russet haired daughter of Dublin,
Fierce foremother to poets wise and brave,
You knew the tenuous path of women through
the rain-beaten loam of Ireland's history.
You fathomed how far a woman's station falls,
Only to disappear under the waves of this island's slate green waters,
Sunken treasure, lost among the bard-worthy battles of kings, men
and nationhood.

You declared the charwoman's labors and the proud
march in red of the women of the pave,
As worthy of praise as the great heroes of Ireland,
with their cries for independence.
For you are Ireland and history too.

We lost you during dark days
in a time of plague. You watched as we clasped
our rose-scented babes at dawn and felt the wear of time
in the night feeds during our longest hours.

You sang to those starved and beaten, while raising the almost broken,
The half-souls and the dead, you chronicled those lost in
the fog of forgetting, when no one recollected our names.
So you called upon our ancestral spirits to sit with us again today,
as twilight falls upon our kitchen tables.

It is an ancient grief to mourn the loss of a poet,
To mourn for more words,
For more comfort from a stilled pen.
For you visited us within your pages
And we are not forgotten.

"Women of the pave" is Irish slang for "ladies of the night."

Dream After Reading Richard Wilbur
Sally Ridgway

I travel to an island for a workshop, to an old house
in the hunks and colors of a painting off the coast
of Maine.

       To my host and her husband in their khakis.
It's my second year and I have a job to do.

               But first
she shows me a photo—a blurry black and white taken
in their bedroom. She's looking down at him,

                  tender
and serene. *My soul hangs for a moment.* Yet in a hush
of *bitter love* she says it's hard, married

             to a hunter. And
he keeps not answering my question of his last bird's
name. *"They rose together in calm swells so quiet nobody
seemed to be there,"* he muses.

         Then *in a changed voice*
tells of his difficult obsession—the birds, those spirits
of air flying *in the sight of heaven.*

         His wife and I leave
for her enormous blue desk with its strewn papers
and mystery of cubbyholes and

        drawers I want to open.
But *my soul shrinks* remembering my job. I must gather
clean linens for our guests.

       From *outside the open window,*

a cry of pulleys. That angel Richard Wilbur is hanging white *bed-sheets* on a line.

Birds Never Nest Here

T. R. Poulson

to Richard Hugo and his book, Triggering Town

You've never heard of my town. It straddles
Forgotten River, where the Main Street Trestle
once crossed. It's now gone, and a ferry paddles
back and forth, Sundays. On the west
side stands the butcher's shop, the tenderest meats,
on the east, his wife picks grapes and cherries,
bakes pies to feed her other lover, a concrete
mixer. We're all believers here, where barges carry
guests of every faith to downtown docks.
We put down pillows and towels in spare
guest rooms, serve pancakes, and the ancient books.
We pray. Those who don't repent just disappear.
It's a mystery where the butcher finds his prey,
the nearest ranch, four hundred miles away.

Pablo Wrote a Word
Mary Horner

to Pablo Medina

When Pablo wrote a word,
He confessed the language
of my birth was all he had to
keep him warm at night.
That was when I began to
look for him inside the syllables of
brevity and confinement, and on the internet.

Pablo plays among beautiful sentences
that crawl back and forth between
Foreign nouns and verbs that have no
connection except that he strung them
Together along the precarious
Verge of hope and sorrow.

He stretches words between both
Homes with a mind that collects shells
Without knowing what resides in them.
In the last phrase before winding
Down and settling for, a key word can
Leave him with a different patois.

How Could You Write in Dickinson's Room?

Connie Ann Kirk

to Emily Dickinson

To be entirely honest, it was the light
that kept me in that room, her space,
my time, and yes; I did have a deep,
once deepening sense of guilt — but
vanity of curiosity won. I wanted to see
how light — from the exact same sun —
even on a day when it hid its face, may
have illuminated her delicate, pocket-
sized pages with brilliance, fired her mind,
brightened her words in that space,
same space, this

space.
Was it catching? Could I bottle it,
take it home with me to my room,
my time? Was a certain slant
of light, after all
that struggle,
the one and true pure answer?

The Good Woman Travels Lightly
Susan Swartwout

to Lucille Clifton

A good woman dies, sifts into the earth,
lifetime by molecule, payment made
on a ticket purchased at birth.

The woman's travel brochure is succinct:
unpack your veil of blood and gutstrings,
your blanketing layers of fur and flake,
that teaming planet that incorporates
whatever you call yourself
to yourself today

Body is a basket of bonekindling and root
vegetables soft as a bruised heart,
a gathering of busy compost
to be raked and arranged,
dampened and dug
over careless decades.
To launch your flight,
set down that trug, drift
into the heavier air
like a bright balloon, waving
so-long to the dust —
your only tie,
a string
of poems

Desire Is a Tangled Beast
Christine Rhein

to Mary Jo Firth Gillett

Desire is the bag lady
who calls to you by name,
hands you an old matchbook,
whispers *It's a plane ticket.*

Desire's engine runs counter-
clockwise.
Clock *wise*,
desire makes its own chime.

When desire plays
a steel guitar, the song bares
and bears each chord,
every tremor.

Desire shakes its cocktails,
wants that rhinestone sparkle,
spirits electric red.

Everyone bellies up to the glow
of desire, sporting the latest
in chameleon fashion,
hibiscus tease.

When desire writes poetry, it's mad
for enjambment, movement
both free and formal.

Desire pretends not to crave more
of itself. But it keeps reflecting
on Escher's drawn hands
drawing each other into being.

Desire knows sunrise and sunset
are the same door, unhinging.

Stumbling into desire
leads to sinking
in quicksand in a jungle on an island
in a parallel world.

Someday there will be a quantum
theory of desire, all bets off
when you're not looking.

Torn and Resolved
Amanda Giles

> *"There will come a time when I must face myself at last."*
> Sylvia Plath, Letters to Roman

Oh, to write like Sylvia Plath
To embrace her sorrows and ply her wrath

So, to harness her syntax powers
Crafting a work that stings and flowers

Grow, to capture and to compose
Intricate poetry, heart-rending prose

Lo, to blend the spectre of death
With tulips and bees — empowering breath

Go, to seek this Lazarus Maid
Who plaited her thoughts into a noose-braid

Woe, to weather the pangs she felt
I cannot sojourn where Sylvia dwelt

So, to honor her spark and strife
I dictate my path — I unfurl my life

Oh, to share the rain on my face
Like glistening words that fall into place

For Ungaretti: Portrait of the Virile Poet as Senex

Pellegrino A. D'Acierno

to Giuseppe Ungaretti

We need used words to modify our youth
tracing in us Adam's intact desire.
We need the old man's remembering
to bring us to our beginning
by devouring his archaic dreams —

dead desert mirages animating . . .
meridian fables, satyr-words
pastorals of desire . . .
trees of dense shade nymphs incarna-
   ting . . .
dream ikons into present distance ab-
   stracting . . .
carnality of dreams opening . . .

We need the old man to beget in us an
   aurora
shattering the secularity of repetition —

  originating dawn,
  apocalyptic dawn instressing Adam's
  day,
  binding us to the commencement,
  waking mind to the day's ideal body.

We need the old man to recover
our antique rhythms —

  physiology of lost rhythms . . .
  subtraction from anterior silence,

syllable added into song,
endecassillabo, sestina enduring our an-
archy,
liberating us into the obedience of time.
Word within a word
Dance within a dance
Penelope within a star

The poet measures secret into secret,
mediates through a glass of words
inequalities of light —
incipient star and Baroque sun.
The ascesis of hyperbole: to carry the sun
        in a cup.
The poet keeps the dawn pure,
sees suffered into cyclical stone of universe
the beginning sensuality of woman's face
        and diffuse curve —
nuptiality of morning.
The poet cannot forget remembering —
here Phaedrus and everything already echo
and even silence an interruption.
The poet remembering continues us,
remembering Christ into unicorn of pity,
stars into fables bereft of Odysseus,
woman into a tree of dream,
figures absolute of silence into
gracious fingers of word and rose.
Landscape is not rhetorical,
the world is not invented,
no paraphrases of the sun.
The sun is an epiphany loosened
into its own language — suddenly.
Innocence is not a myth or a preceding myth
or what an Adam-dark dream constructs,
but the Dream itself . . .
circumference, precinct of light,

mask of light,
emblem forever doubling our first images.

Once upon a time
Blazing a beginning analogy
Ungaretti perpetual in the sun –
Repose of sun.

Feast
Mike Graves

to James Wright

While prowling in bookstores,
  I remember the names of authors
You penciled in the margins
In your cramped hand —
Remember them always.
One by one,
I find them and feast,
Feast like a savage
Eating his totem
To feel it within,
Take on its power,
Merge and restore
Memory, elf,
And the word,
"The pure, clear word."

The Word Man: Ode to Teacher, Poet, Priest

Betty Kort

to My Friend Chuck Peek

"Let not many of you become teachers, my brethren, for you know that we who teach shall be judged with greater strictness . . . Look at the ships also; though they are so great and are driven by strong winds, they are guided by a very small rudder wherever the will of the pilot directs . . . So [too] the tongue is a little member and boasts of great things." (James 3: 1-5)

In a bookstore in our town
Volumes scattered all around
Stands a kind and stalwart man
Respected as a keen observer
Stretching up, reaching down
Mumbling titles
Pointing fingers
Touching bindings here and there

He's a *word* man,
That's for certain
Some would say a master poet
Voicing wisdom's art and treasure

Massive texts trail in his wake
Each with careful, measured diction
Honed to fit his firm intention
And avoid miscalculation
Books and poems, awards and praise
Blogs to treasure, quotes to gauge
Verse reflecting human nature

Priest and friend, colleague, mentor
Teacher with the will to lead

Deep-set love and warming grace
Nourish countless hungry souls

With quiet mien and careful logic
He uses language like a scalpel
Carves through pretext cloaked in valor
Destroys deceits and petty falsehood
And urges truth to starboard

He's a word man, that's for certain
Acclaimed as writer, cleric, scholar
Ordained to teach and to recite
Splendid verse with power and might

The White Farmhouse
Stuart P. Radowitz

to Robert Frost

The farmhouse was white, surrounded
thirteen acres, mostly open, some wooded.
A small pond, an acre and a half
in the back, a well
one hundred fifty feet deep.

Drinking water flowed up
from an ancient underground stream.
Deer knew it was a safe place to graze.
A red fox often loped by,
as if going somewhere.

When you said hello this morning,
I kissed your shoulder.
Our house is warm, though in the winter
it was not always so.

Thursday a gray dove landed under the white pine.
She was looking for a safe place to die.
Friday morning she had moved nearer to the pond
to a place where two sections of fence meet.

When you said good night I went out,
put my finger in the well and touched
the rough damp brick.

The red fox came by again
but did not touch the dove.
No one was hungry enough to eat.

While the Two of Us Were Breathing
Ulf Kirchdorfer

for Seamus Heaney

Gray-haired, with a haircut that would never have been allowed
in my house, you came to a fine room reserved for special occasions,
by chance another student and I were invited by our professor to join,
and we sat on huge, comfortable sofas, the talk first a little uncomfort-
    able,
then friendly without any sense that you were paid to be on campus,
and my professor asked if I had any poetry to read, which of course I
    had
but back in my dorm room, and I ran the fastest I have ever, returning
    with
one or two sheets, and your warm voice praised what I had written,
but also without threat or condescension told me I might want to fix
"human imagination's moral perversion," "a bit of a mouthful,' and this
was all before I knew how famous you were and I had explained to you
that the seven white dogs sitting on dolomite mountains were the seven
sacraments, something I had picked up and inserted half-digested,
and then over the years came kind post cards with your self-effacing
    humor.

After Watching Leaves Fall
Like Rain from the Maples
David James

to Galway Kinnell

The end is in sight

when the entire front yard
is buried in yellow leaves. November
arrives this weekend, right

on schedule. Nothing we do
can slow the clock, jar
the minute hand and stop the fall.

My parents are moving in with us
for the winter, failing health, their ten acres too hard
to keep up when my dad can't make it

fifty feet without resting. It's a small
sacrifice for the people who gave me everything.
My wife's mom is in the hospital, critical care,

after finding liquid around her heart when they went to install
a new pacemaker. There's nothing new
to report here: the wheel turns, crushes a few, brings

us all, eventually, to the end of the hallway.
The lights dim, the room collapses into one last piece
of good air, the body grows a pair of wings

and whispers, "I quit."

To W.S.: My Rage for Order
Terrell Tebbetts

to Wallace Stevens

In my mattress microscopic mites
dine, I read, on flakes of skin
I slough into their jaws each night,

and from the tell-tale dung I'd say
a bat is snuggling in the ceiling
of my porch each topsy-turvy day.

I've wakened when a cat in heat
was crouched beneath my house
wailing for the tom across the street.

Sometimes I've seen a sparrow flit
with crickets for its hungry
fledglings chirping in my soffit.

Each evening, though invading vermin
and waking bats and creatures wild
with hunger howl and growl within,

at suppertime we five still face
each other at our table, bow
our heads, and start our meal with grace,

and every day I carpenter what lines
I can into this house of life.

Tribute to Gerard Manley Hopkins

Barbara Novack

Melancholy priest
passion pouring from your pen
denying darkness in your mind
happiness on your lips
only as you died.

Oh, melancholy priest
how much joy
your words provide.

"In the Presence of the Marvelous"
Cindy Frenkel

to Molly Peacock

I'm invisible — and my mouth is zipped.
It's England, the late eighteenth century.
Mary Delany sits in luxury,
alone. I observe her precisely snip
a crisp paper, place it — a ruffled tulip —
on a black background. At her apogee,
she's seventy-two, making history.
Immersed in her world, I'm in the backdrop

of this widow who invents collage. I
notice she cuts a frill of iris, piece
by piece orders her life, lets the paint dry,
gingerly layers bud on vine, each crease
smoothed smartly by her firm hand and honed eye,
life created anew — my own release.

(Title excerpted from p. 229 of *The Paper Garden* by Molly Peacock)

Differences We Know/Not
J. F. DeVoe

to Amanda Gorman

We, the privileged unknown . . . unaware of
Our stories were washed — with history missing and facts misslead-
ing: Tuskegee, Tulsa and tomahawk Tales.

Filthy rich, immigrant poor
Us/them, there too close, here too far
Of a kind theirs and ours, draw the line.

Schools divided, Sports collided
Boys along the wall, girls across to the other
Catholic clear — there's only One
White bearded He is, yet Popes can come in pairs
Jesus the Jew, the Sun colored Son.

Maternal impressions matter most, from the get Go to No.
Mine amplified us,
Our styles, smiles . . . walk, talk . . . and being "better than".
Mothers know even with Identicals: skills & thrills, words & won-
ders, dreams & lies — the sames, The odds and better thans.

Moments are times that live once, caught or lost . . .
In this, with that, out there for those
Who feast, on and off the street, (rarely) complete
To Be, or simply pose . . .
Moms teach with touch, that any pebble, droplet, flower or beast and
everybody is a hue
Of one another, not simply a colorless rose.

Paternal shadows tower over absent hours . . .
Dads push the games, prompt the practice, promise success — if
we're better than.
Compete through the finish line — no retreat

Complete the incomplete — no defeat.

Offer without being asked,
Order in order, counting to be ready and right.

Look up to the stars, Look down for the ground
Leave fast, stay long and win again - and again.

One should lead, still join . . . cause it's a team tally
Only one to a role, belief over doubt, in front for the rally.

Remember,
At night, who's who — neither wrong, nor a fright.

In the light,
You're someone new I never knew — Who's inspired me anew.

Special, better and different than
You're another player to challenge, yet cherish . . . without Whom
There's no game, no glory
Little to learn, less to gain
And life's a blind ride over the same.

Pennies for Pilgrims
Julie Allyn Johnson

to Annie Dillard

Beneath a cumulonimbus-filled Sunday sky, I'm relaxed, hands
folded low across my scrunched-in tummy, last season's capri pants
(loads of pockets) pulled in tight so as to fasten both the button and
the zip but by God, I made it work. I've got all summer to rid myself
of these pandemic pounds. Eyes closed against the white brightness,
I 'lax and take it all in: the chitters and chirps, occasional hum of
a small plane overhead, cooling breeze to ease the rising temps and
hint of humidity. A sudden burst of avian whooping and hollering:
something or someone getting too close, methinks. Opening my eyes,
I catch sight of oriole orange gliding into the upper reaches of our
little leaf linden. On the western skyline, a foursome wanders off the
third green, all but one of them seemingly content with their efforts
thus far, just in time to hook up with the Beer Babe though doubtful
they have Michelob in mind this early in the day. Then again, I could
be wrong. Puffs of cottonwood float above me with abandon — each
one hoping, hoping . . . A car door slams, then another, followed by
tiny shrieks of laughter and the patter of little feet. From somewhere
down the street, I hear the gentle lawnmower-purr of an industrious
neighbor and it reminds me that I, too, have grass that needs tending.
The world continues to revolve all around us, regardless of the import
we attach to what's happening. Maybe it's better — sometimes —
that we don't. For the moment, I'm satisfied, content in my pursuit of
a *healthy poverty*, the *simplicity* of joys where — and when — I find
them.

Kate Light
John Aicher

to Kate Light

Miss Kate's buoy
rings its winter bell,
her hair laying an icy
flow into swells
rising in greeting
falling in troughs
seabirds float through.
Freezing hair dangling
in waves chambers
hope that Spring
may carry her
from mooring
to minds at sea
rhythmically.

Index of Echoes

Index to Tributes

Contributors

John Aicher is a practicing attorney on Long Island. A graduate of Middlebury College and New York Law School, he has been an avid sportsman in baseball and football, and, in his younger days, an ocean lifeguard. John is also a private pilot and, besides writing poetry, he paints watercolors. When stressed in law school, he would visit 4 Patchin Place, New York City, where e e cummings lived. (72, 167)

Dee Allen is an African-Italian performance poet based in Oakland, California. Active on the creative writing & Spoken Word tips since the early 1990s, he is the author of five books—*Boneyard, Unwritten Law, Stormwater, Skeletal Black*, and, most recently, *Elohi Unitsi*. His work has also been included in numerous anthologies."Frontline Hero" was originally published in the newspaper, *Street Spirit*. (31, 109)

Lana Hechtman Ayers, night-owl, coffee-enthusiast, author of nine poetry collections and a time travel novel, lives on the north Oregon coast where she enjoys the near-constant plunk of rain on the roof and the sea's steady whoosh. Visit her online at LanaAyers.com. (46, 126)

Allen Braden, who was raised on a family farm in the Pacific Northwest and now lives in Lakewood, Washington, is the author of *A Wreath of Down and Drops of Blood* and *Elegy in the Passive Voice*. His work has appeared in numerous anthologies or textbooks, including *The Bedford Introduction to Literature, Best New Poets, New Poets of the American West*, and *Poetry: An Introduction*. Both of his poems included here appear in *Elegy in the Passive Voice*. (49, 128)

Lynne Burnett lives on Vancouver Island. Her poems have been published in *American Journal of Poetry, Arc Poetry, Blue Heron Review, Comstock Review*, and other journals and anthologies. A Best of the Net and Pushcart nominee, she is a winner of the Lauren K. Alleyne Difficult Fruit Poetry Prize and Jack Grapes Poetry Prize. Visit her at https://lynneburnett.ca/. Both of the poems in this anthology were published in her chapbook *Irresistible*. (53, 133)

Ann Cefola, who lives in the New York suburbs, is the author of *Free Ferry* and *Face Painting in the Dark*, and translator of Hélène Sanguinetti's *The Hero and Hence This Cradle*. (52, 132)

Carolyn Chatham is a San Antonio poet whose poetry has appeared in several anthologies and quarterlies including San Antonio's *30 Poems for the Tricentennial, The Texas Poetry Calendar, Voices de la Luna,* and others, and in her book, *Those Bones that Float About.* A member of Sun Poet Society, she is currently working on a book of speculative fiction. Her poems in this anthology were originally published in *Those Bones that Float About.* (57, 138)

Misty McCormick Chisum, an English instructor who now lives in Vermont, often writes about growing up in the Missouri Bootheel region. The two poems included here illustrate the rural tie to the land—from birth to death— and the weight of the struggles between. (44, 124)

Geraldine Connolly is the author of a chapbook and four poetry collections, including the recent *Aileron.* She has taught at the Writers Center in Bethesda, Maryland, the Chautauqua Institution, and the University of Arizona Poetry Center and has received fellowships from the National Endowment for the Arts, the Maryland Arts Council, and the Breadloaf Writers Conference. She lives in Tucson, Arizona. "For Emily" was published in *SWWIM Journal*; "Being a Female" is included in *Aileron.* (38, 117)

David R. Cravens received his undergraduate degree in philosophy at the University of Missouri, and his master's in English at Southeast Missouri State University. He has won the Saint Petersburg Review Prize in Poetry, and the Bedford Poetry Prize. His work appears in literary journals throughout the U.S. and abroad. (24, 107)

Pellegrino D'Acierno is Distinguished Professor Emeritus of Comparative Literature and Italian Studies at Hofstra University and a Senior Scholar at Columbia University. He is the author of three books of poetry: *The Fat Man Arpeggios, Thirteen Ways of Crossing the Piazza: Collected Poems*, and *Anti-Haiku Moments and Profane Illuminations: The Exorbitance of Italy* (forthcoming). (74, 152)

Todd Davis is the author of six collections of poetry, most recently *Native Species* and *Winterkill.* His writing has won the Foreword INDIES Book of the Year Bronze and Silver Awards, the Gwendolyn Brooks Poetry Prize, the Chautauqua Editors Prize, and the Bloomsburg University Book Prize. He teaches environmental studies, American literature, and creative writing at Pennsylvania State University's Altoona College. Both "Dead Letter to Elizabeth Bishop" and "Dead Letter to Richard Hugo" appear in Native Species. (14, 96)

J. F. DeVoe, after an accomplished 40-year career in educational publishing, is learning to grandparent, engage in adult parenting, and relish time with his soul mate, Sylvia. Reading and writing, risky handicapping and politicking, and daily organic eating are all part of his day punctuated by QiGong exercises. (85, 164)

Nicholas Fargnoli is dean emeritus of humanities, professor of English at Molloy College in Rockville Centre, NY; recently, he stepped down as president of the James Joyce Society, a position he held for over 20 years. He has published on James Joyce and William Faulkner and in the field of contemporary ethics. (25, 111)

Sandy Feinstein teaches at Penn State Berks in Reading, Pennyslvania. Her poems have appeared most recently in *Zingara* and *Maximum Tilt*. A chapbook of her poems, Swimming to Syria, is forthcoming. Earlier her poems responding to Shakespeare appeared in the Iowa anthology, *A Fine Frenzy*. Her courses incorporate creative projects where students devise ways to make early and contemporary literature their own. (16, 105)

Cindy Frenkel, of Huntington Woods, Michigan, has an M.F.A. from Columbia University and has served as a Writer-in-Residence with InsideOut Literary Arts Project (iO), which brings working poets into Detroit public schools. She is the author of *The Plague of the Tender-Hearted*, and her work has appeared in publications ranging from *Writers in Education* to *Vanity Fair* to *WIRED online* and in the anthologies *Divining Dante* and *To Light a Fire*. To learn more, visit www. cindyfrenkel.com. (84, 163)

Carly Lynn Gates is a communication arts teacher at a public arts high school in South Florida. She holds an MFA in creative writing from the University of the South's School of Letters. She has also been an MFA scholar at the Sewanee Writers' Conference. Her poetry has been published in *Flint Hills Review*, *Hawai'i Review*, and *So to Speak*, among others, and is forthcoming in the anthology *Pantoums for the 21st Century*. "The Writer's Wife" appeared in *What We Talk About When We Talk About It: Variations on the Theme of Love*, Volume One, and in the online edition of *So to Speak*. (56, 136)

Timothy Gauss is the co-founder of *Poet2Poet,* an organization that connects writers through conversation and collaboration. His works cover a broad spectrum of genres including poetry, fantasy, graphic novels, animated film, and children's books. In truth, Timothy wholeheartedly believes in the magic of imagination and approaches his writing with the same tenacity and sense of wonder as his penchant for jaunty hats. (32, 103)

Amanda Giles is a school librarian and guitar instructor with a degree in Human Development. She lives with her husband and three children in Washington County, Oregon. She is happiest when exploring a nature park, photographing flowers, or diving into her latest library book. (73, 151)

Mike Graves has published several books of poetry including *A Prayer for the Less Violent Offenders: The Selected Short Poems of Mike Graves*. A new volume of poems titled *Preparing the Apology* is forthcoming. He also organizes poetry readings in New York City and on Staten Island. (76, 155)

Robert Hamblin is a professor emeritus of English and founding director of the Center for Faulkner Studies at Southeast Missouri State University, where he taught for 50 years. He has authored or edited 47 books, including *Epiphanies Large and Small: Collected Poems* and *Mississippi and Beyond: Selected Essays.* "Traveling" and "What I Would Have Said to Seamus Heaney" originally appeared in *Mind the Gap: Poems by an American in London.* (21, 93)

Mary Horner, an adjunct faculty member at St. Louis Community College and the former managing editor of the Journal of the American Optometric Association, is the author of *Strengthen Your Nonfiction Writing* and blogger for *WOW! Women on Writing*. She currently serves as a reader for Boulevard, and her poetry, stories, and essays have been published in several journals and anthologies. "Pablo Wrote a Word" was originally published in *Mid Rivers Review.* (67, 146)

D. R. James has taught college writing, literature, and peace-making for 36 years and lives in the woods near Saugatuck, Michigan. His most recent of nine collections are *Flip Requiem, Surreal Expulsion*, and *If god were gentle*, and his micro-chapbook *All Her Jazz* is free, fun, and printable-for-folding at the Origami Poems Project. "Songs of the Sirens of Life" first appeared in *Peacock Journal.* (35, 112)

David James teaches writing at Oakland Community College in Michigan. His most recent books, *A Gem of Truth* and *Nail Yourself into Bliss*, came out in 2019. More than thirty of his one-act plays have been produced in the U.S. and Ireland. (82, 160)

Don Johnson has published four books of poetry, the last of which is *More Than Heavy Rain*, as well as a novel, *Blue Winged Olive*, and various articles on sport literature and contemporary poetry. After 30+ years as a faculty member at East Tennessee State University (the last ten as Poet in Residence), he is living in retirement on the Watauga River in east Tennessee. For 20 years he was an editor of *Aethlon: the Journal of Sport Literature*. "Letter to Longley from the River House" was published in *Hampton Sydney Review* and in *More Than Heavy Rain*. "Muskrat" also appears in *More Than Heavy Rain*. (41, 119)

Julie Allyn Johnson, a sawyer's daughter from north central Iowa, loves hiking, gravel-travel photography, riding bikes, altered books and collage, reading and writing poetry and exploring trails in the Rocky Mountains. Her work has been published in *Typishly, Chestnut Review, The Loch Raven Review, Typehouse Literary Magazine, Into the Void, The Briar Cliff Review,* and other journals. "Isosceles" first appeared in *Kitchen Sink Magazine*, and "Pennies for Pilgrims" was originally published in *The Metaworker Literary Magazine*. (86, 166)

Ulf Kirchdorfer is a poet and bird photographer who lives in Georgia. He is the author of three books, the latest being a book of poems, *Hamlet in Exile*; co-editor of a book of humorous poetry; and a Faulkner aficionado. "Hamlet of My Childhood" was first published in a slightly different version in *Hamlet in Exile* (Lamar University Literary Press, 2020). The Seamus Heaney tribute is part of a collection "Icarus Plays Scrabble," a work in progress. (81, 159)

Connie Ann Kirk holds a Ph.D. in Creative Writing and Literature from Binghamton University. The author of several non-fiction books, including *Emily Dickinson: A Biography*, she is the recipient of an artist's grant for her poetry from the New York State Council on the Arts. (68, 147)

Betty Kort, as an English and art teacher, was named the 1993 Nebraska Teacher of the Year. Following her teaching career, she served first as Executive Director of the Willa Cather Foundation and later as Executive Director of the Hastings Public Schools Foundation. Her photography has been widely exhibited in the United States under the sponsorship of the National Endowment for the Arts; and her work was celebrated with a major exhibit in 2021 in Nebraska featuring 30 paintings and mixed media pieces, each accompanied by her poetry. (77, 156)

Jim LaVilla-Havelin is the author of five books of poetry, the most recent of which is *WEST, Poems of a Place*. He is the San Antonio Coordinator of National Poetry Month activities and calendar, and the poetry editor for the *San Antonio Express-News/Houston Chronicle*. (55, 135)

Carey Link is from Huntsville, Alabama. Her poetry has previously appeared in *Birmingham Poetry Review, Poem, Hospital Drive*, and elsewhere. Carey has published two poetry collections, *What It Means to Climb a Tree* and *Awakening to Holes in the Arc of Sun*. "The Last Stage" previously appeared in *The Valley Weekly*. "My Time" is included in *Awakening to Holes in the Arc of Sun*. (42, 121)

Peter Ludwin is the recipient of a Literary Fellowship from Artist Trust and a past winner of the Muriel Craft Bailey Memorial Award from *The Comstock Review*. His most recent book, *Gone to Gold Mountain*, was nominated for both a Washington State Book Award and an American Book Award. A frequent participant in The San Miguel Poetry Week in Mexico, he works for a local nonprofit that helps immigrant farmers grow organic food for themselves and the community. "Remembering Theodore Roethke after a Return to the University of Washington" was published in *Slant*. "On a Landscape Job You Pour New Wine into Old Skins" appeared in *Soundings Review*. (51, 130)

M. L. Lyons studied Creative Writing at the University of Washington and Publishing at Simon Fraser University. After interning at Copper Canyon Press, she co-edited *Raising Lilly Ledbetter: Women Poets Occupy the Workplace* with Carolyne Wright and Eugenia Toledo. Her poetry has been nominated for the *Pushcart* and most recently she received a VorTEXT scholarship from Hedgebrook writers' residency. (62, 142)

Carolyn Martin has moved from associate professor of English to management trainer to retiree. A lover of gardening and snorkeling, feral cats and backyard birds, writing and photography, she has recently published her fourth poetry collection, A Penchant for Masquerades. You may find out more about her at www.carolynmartinpoet.com. "Shall I compare thee to a summer's day?" was first published in Antiphon; "You do not have to be good" appeared in Gyroscope Review. (34, 106)

Kevin McIlvoy lives in Asheville, North Carolina. His most recent books are *At the Gate of All Wonder, 57 Octaves Below Middle C*, and *One Kind Favor*. He has published poems in *Scoundrel Time, Barzakh*, and *River Heron Review*. The two poems appearing here are from a book in progress, *The River Scratch*. (17, 90)

Barbara Novack is Writer-in-Residence and member of the English Department at Molloy College. Her books include the novel *J.W. Valentine*, nominated for a Pulitzer Prize and finalist for Pushcart Press Editor's Book Award, the full-length poetry collections, *Something Like Life* and *Dancing on the Rim of Light*, and two chapbooks, *Do Houses Dream?* and *A Certain Slant of Light*, both finalists for the Blue Light Press Poetry Prize. (83, 162)

Charles A. Peek has taught at four universities, helped Bob Hamblin write two books, served as Rector of several Episcopal Churches, and raised a family. His *Breezes on their Way to Being Winds* won the a Nebraska Book Award for Poetry. His most recent book is *Nebraska~Conflicting Reports*. (40, 118)

James Penha, a native New Yorker, has lived for the past quarter-century in Indonesia. Nominated for Pushcart Prizes in fiction and poetry, his verse recently appeared in *Headcase: LGBTQ Writers & Artists on Mental Health* and *Wellness, Lovejets: queer male poets on 200 years of Walt Whitman*, and *What Remains: The Many Ways We Say Goodbye*. His essays have appeared in *The New York Daily News* and *The New York Times*. Penha edits The New Verse News, an online journal of current-events poetry."Red and White: Can the Blues Be Far Behind?" was published in *Defining Moments: The Plymouth Writers Group Anthology* 9; "Digging Lorca" appeared in *New Verse News*. (26, 104)

T. R. Poulson, a University of Nevada alum and proud Wolf Pack fan, lives in San Mateo, California. Her work has appeared in several journals, including *Rattle, Booth, Verdad, Trajectory, The Meadow, Alehouse, Raintown Review, New Verse News, Aethlon: The Journal of Sport Literature*, and *J Journal*. (66, 145)

Stuart P. Radowitz, a Brooklyn-born and -raised Long Island poet, is an instructor in the English Department at Molloy College. He has been widely published in journals, anthologies, and literary magazines; and he has authored a book of poems, *Snow Hangs on the Branches of Evergreens*. "The White Farmhouse" was previously published in *Nassau County Poet Laureate Society Review*. (79, 158)

Christine Rhein is the author of *Wild Flight*, a winner of the Walt McDonald First Book Prize in Poetry (Texas Tech University Press). Her poems have appeared widely in literary journals, including *Southern Review* and *Gettysburg Review*, and have won awards from *Michigan Quarterly Review* and *Green Mountains Review*. Her work has also been published in many anthologies, including *The Best American Nonrequired Reading*. She lives in Brighton, Michigan. "Grief Like Sand" was published on *The American Scholar* website; "Desire Is a Tangled Beast" was published in *The MacGuffin*. (71, 149)

Sally Ridgway has poems in literary journals including *Gulf Coast, Phoebe*, and *Nimrod* and in anthologies such as *Improbable Worlds*; *No Achilles: War Poetry* ; and *The Southern Poetry Anthology*. She has an MFA in Writing from Vermont College and has taught English in Community College, led creative writing workshops, and tutored in poetry writing. (64, 143)

Jack Ridl has published several books of poetry, including *Broken Symmetry* (awarded Year's Best Collection by The Society of Midland/Midwest Authors) , *Losing Season* (named Best Sports Book by The Institute for International Sport), and *Practicing to Walk Like a Heron* (named Year's Best Collection by ForeWord/ Indie Fab Reviews). His latest collection is *Saint Peter and the Goldfinch*. More than 90 of his former students are now publishing. Each Thursday on his website, www.ridl.com, he offers a poem and commentary. "Things Are Never the Same" first appeared in *Talking River Review* and then in *Saint Peter and the Goldfinch*. "Over in That Corner the Puppets" first appeared in *Peninsula Poets* and then in *Saint Peter and the Goldfinch*. (23, 99)

Jeanie Sanders is a poet and collage artist. Her poems have been published in several anthologies, magazines, and newspapers. Her book *The Book of the Dead: Poems and Photographs* is a collection of poetry and photography that seeks to find meaning in mundane and otherwise forgotten lives. (54, 134)

Judith Sanders, who lives in Pittsburgh, is the author of the forthcoming poetry collection *In Deep*. She has published work in journals such as *The American Scholar* and *Calyx,* and on the websites *Vox Populi* and *Full Grown People.* She has won the Hart Crane Poetry Prize and the Wergle Flomp Humor Poetry Prize. She taught English at universities and independent schools, and in France on a Fulbright Fellowship. "The Treat" was published in *The Pittsburgh Post-Gazette* and included in *Ice Cream Poems*, edited by Patricia Fargnoli. "Autumn Walk at Beechwood Farms" appeared on the *Vox Populi* website. (29, 100)

Linda Simone is the author of *The River Will Save Us* and two chapbooks, *Archeology* and *Cow Tippers*. Her work has appeared in *Poets to Come*, a Whitman Bicentennial commemorative anthology. Her poems were selected for the city of San Antonio's Tricentennial and Poet Laureate's signature project. You may find her at www.lindasimone.com. (50, 129)

Ron Smith, Poet Laureate of Virginia, 2014–2016, is the author of *Moon Road, Its Ghostly Workshop, The Humility of the Brutes, Running Again in Hollywood Cemetery* and the forthcoming *The Beauty in the Trees*. His poems have appeared in *The Nation, Georgia Review, Kenyon Review*, and many other periodicals and anthologies in North America and Europe. He is currently Writer-in-Residence at St. Christopher's School in Richmond VA, and the poetry editor for *Aethlon: The Journal of Sport Literature*. "E.P. in the Garden" was first published in *Artemis*. A slightly different version of "The Angry Poem Circling Urban Grit All Night in Search of Tenderness" appeared in *Poultry: A Magazine of Voice*. (59, 140)

Sarah Dickenson Snyder has written poetry since she knew there was a form with conscious line breaks. She has three poetry collections: *The Human Contract, Notes from a Nomad* (nominated for the Massachusetts Book Awards), and *With a Polaroid Camera*. Recently, poems appeared in *Artemis, Sewanee Review*, and *RHINO*. She was accepted twice to the Bread Loaf Writers' Conference, and one poem was selected by the Massachusetts Poetry Festival Migration Contest to be stenciled on the sidewalk in Salem. "For Me, Talking With God" was published in *Panoply*, a literary zine, and "On the Bank" was published in *isacoustic*. (11, 98)

Joseph Stanton is the author of six collections of poems: *Moving Pictures, Things Seen, Imaginary Museum, A Field Guide to the Wildlife of Suburban Oahu, Cardinal Points*, and *What the Kite Thinks*. His other books include *Looking for Edward Gorey, The Important Books: Children's Picture Books as Art and Literature*, and *Stan Musial: A Biography*. He is a Professor Emeritus of Art History and American Studies at University of Hawaii at Manoa. "Storm at Cedarmere" is included in *Moving Pictures* and was also published in *Cortland Review*. "Yorick Replies to Hamlet" appeared in *Mississippi Review*. (12, 95)

Susan Swartwout is the author of the poetry book *Odd Beauty, Strange Fruit*, poetry chapbooks *Freaks and Uncommon Ground*, editor of *Proud to Be: Writing by American Warriors* volumes 1 through 5, and the co-editor of *Hurricane Blues: Poems About Katrina and Rita, Real Things: An Anthology of Popular Culture in American Poetry*, and *A Student's Guide to Publishing*. Besides teaching creative writing and editing, she worked in the publishing industry for 27 years as an editor and copyeditor for various presses and 16 years as a university-press publisher. (70, 148)

Terrell Tebbetts is the Martha Heasley Cox Chair in American Literature at Lyon College. His poems have appeared in a number of literary journals including *Cave Region Review, Elder Mountain, The Lyric, Sparrow, Poet, Whole Notes*, and *Voices International*. (87, 161)

Sheri Vandermolen began composing poetry in 2013, and her work has since been published in dozens of prominent journals, from North America to Southeast Asia. Her book *Jasmine Fractals: Poems of Urban India* captures verse and digital images generated during her six-year residence in Bangalore, and her writing is infused with experiences from her travels to 65 countries. She is also the recipient of multiple photography awards, with gallery display at the Azores Pico Festival and the UK Royal Geographical Society. "Corruption" was published in *Commonline Journal*, and "Seer" appeared in *Verse-Virtual*. (36, 113)

Julene Tripp Weaver is a psychotherapist and writer in Seattle. She has three poetry books: *truth be bold—Serenading Life & Death in the Age of AIDS, No Father Can Save Her*, and a chapbook, *Case Walking: An AIDS Case Manager Wails Her Blues*. She is widely published in journals and anthologies; you can find more of her work online at www.julenetrippweaver.com, and on Twitter @trippweavepoet. "How I Came to This World" was published in *The Seattle Review of Books*. (43, 122)

Philip Wedge is a senior lecturer in English at the University of Kansas and editor of *Cottonwood Magazine and Press*. His work has previously appeared in *Aethlon: the Journal of Sport Literature, The American Scholar, High Plains Literary Review*, and *Kansas Quarterly*, among others. "Deaf and Blind" first appeared in *The American Scholar*. "Lone Star" first appeared in *Coal City Review*. (61, 141)

Anne Harding Woodworth is the author of *Trouble*, her seventh book. She is co-chair of the Poetry Board at the Folger Shakespeare Library in Washington, D.C., where she lives; and she is a member of the Board of Governors of the Emily Dickinson Museum in Amherst, Massachusetts. "Letter from an Old Poet" is in her book *Unattached Male*. (37, 114)

Made in United States
Orlando, FL
12 February 2022

14754306R00109